DISCOVERING
VINTAGE
Boston

A Guide to the City's Timeless Shops, Bars, Restaurants & More

First Edition

MARIA OLIA

Guilford, Connecticut

All the information in this guidebook is subject to change. We recommend that you call ahead to obtain current information before traveling.

An imprint of Rowman & Littlefield
Distributed by NATIONAL BOOK NETWORK

British Library Cataloguing in Publication Information available
Library of Congress Cataloging-in-Publication data available

ISBN 978-1-4930-0646-5

∞™ The paper used in this publication meets the minimum requirements of American National Standard for Information Sciences—Permanence of Paper for Printed Library Materials, ANSI/NISO Z39.48-1992.

Contents

Other Vintage Spots Around Boston

For Masoud, Bijan, Kian, Cameron, and Leda

About the Author

Maria Olia is a travel writer and essayist. Her writing has appeared in the *Boston Globe* and *Working Mother* and many other publications. She has also written *Day Trips New England* and *Insiders' Guide to Massachusetts* for Globe Pequot Press.

Like so many, Maria came to Boston to attend college and never left. She still enjoys being a tourist in her adopted hometown, taking a special interest in the city's performing arts and restaurant scene. She lives with her husband in the city of Newton, just outside of Boston, and is happiest when her three grown sons and daughter come back to their childhood home to visit.

Acknowledgments

When I was first asked to write *Discovering Vintage Boston*, I was thrilled with the idea of sharing Boston's landmark restaurants, shops, and bars. I first visited Boston as a small child—my mother's family has lived here for three generations and I have called Boston home for more than 30 years. I can't imagine living anywhere else.

I am grateful most of all to the business owners who generously gave of their time and allowed me to interview them. Their stories and experiences are the backbone of this book.

Writing this book turned out to be an opportunity to explore some of my hometown's places that I have taken for granted. Many of the 50 spots highlighted here are vestiges of an older Boston: the communal dining tables at Durgin Park; Phillips Candy House, where you can still buy "opera boxes" of chocolates sized to take with you to the theater; and classic thin-crust pizza made in the 1888 brick oven at Regina's in the North End. I won't take these places for granted anymore.

I want to thank my parents, Robert Dascanio and Josephine Sullivan Dascanio, for their support. Even today, in much of Boston being Italian or Irish (especially) still prevails. More so than with any of my other writing projects, my dual ethnicity has served me well.

In the special-mention category, my friend Amy Segal stands out for being a wise sounding board during our daily walks around Crystal Lake.

To my children, Bijan, Kian, Cameron, and Leda: thanks for letting me be your mom and turning out to be such interesting adults. This time around, I am especially grateful to Leda for cheering me on and for pretending to like supermarket rotisserie chicken for way too many dinners. Finally, I am forever thankful to my husband, Masoud, for having the patience for me taking on yet another book project and understanding that I need lots of time to write.

Introduction

What is it about Boston that makes us love it so? For one thing, it's history. Bostonians are tremendously proud of the city's pivotal role in the struggle for American independence. In downtown, where colonial burying grounds, white-spired churches, and redbrick meeting houses are framed by 21st-century skyscrapers, history is evident on practically every street. For Bostonians too, our world-renowned universities, cultural institutions, and even (or especially) our sports teams all enjoy almost mythical stature in our hearts and minds.

Nearly four centuries of stories and legends bind us to this place, founded in 1630 by English Puritans. Boston's annual Patriots' Day celebration is one of those cherished traditions—the 2013 Boston Marathon bombing attack notwithstanding. Every year, on the third Monday of April, the city commemorates the Battles of Lexington and Concord with a reenactment of Paul Revere's ride, the running of the Boston Marathon, and an early Red Sox game. It's a magnificent Boston day.

Frank Lloyd Wright once famously said of Boston, "Clear out 800,000 people and preserve it as a museum piece." Wright got it wrong. One of the city's great paradoxes is that despite being one of the oldest cities in the country, Boston continues to embrace the new. Nearly a quarter million students call Boston home, making the city one of the country's youngest metropolitan areas.

It's not at all surprising that Boston's historic heritage has been preserved. If you're looking for a place to start, walk the 2.5-mile Freedom Trail that links 16 of the city's colonial-era sights. When you're ready for a break from sightseeing, you'll find that many of Boston's most iconic experiences have a bit of history too, and date from earlier times. You can take a ride on a Swan Boat in the Public Garden (1870), catch a game at Fenway Park (1912), or attend a Boston Pops concert (1885). All of these places have endured.

However, Boston is much more than its landmarks and museums. Vintage Boston offers a different view of the city's rich and long history. This book is all about Boston's classic shops, bars, and restaurants. The novelty of certain old spots—places like a tobacconist, a pen shop, and a 24-hour diner—is that they haven't changed, and therefore now feel increasingly special.

Vintage Boston is not so much about the city as it is, but as it was. The 50 places highlighted in this book are all located within Boston or in the neighboring cities of Cambridge and Brookline and range in age from 36 years old to over 270. All have weathered economic downturns, location changes, ownership transfers, and changing customer tastes. Each found its own way to staying power. Some, like the Union Oyster House (1742) and the Warren Tavern (1780), are among the city's most historic and long-standing business enterprises. Others, like Rubin's Kosher Delicatessen (1920), Frank's Steakhouse (1938), and Cheapo Records (1948), are of a decidedly more recent vintage. What they all have in common is that in some way, each place evokes what Boston is all about. Taken together, these spots also trace the city's growth in terms of population and geography. In the years after the Revolutionary War, Boston's economy was based on shipping—and Boston's earliest surviving businesses are the taverns near the waterfront that served the sailors and dockhands. Early industrialization in the 19th century drew Europeans, especially Irish, Italian, and Jewish immigrant groups that settled in the city's neighborhoods: Dorchester, the North End, and the city of Brookline. A growing merchant class in the late 18th century gave rise to hotels, restaurants, and shops in the heart of downtown and in Cambridge.

In a way, this book is a guide to the living landmarks of Boston. As well, each of these shops and restaurants truly represents the idea of buying local—long before there ever was a "movement." These places have not only been around, but are planning to stay around awhile longer. They are all worth visiting.

BETTY ANN FOOD SHOP

565 BENNINGTON ST. • EAST BOSTON, MA 02128

(617) 567-1479

Traditional Doughnuts from an Old-School Bakery

This cute corner bakery on a busy stretch of street in East Boston quietly turns out some of the best doughnuts found anywhere. The shop's window displays both the Stars and Stripes and the Union Jack—an anomaly in this mostly Hispanic neighborhood. Both the baker and his inventory have British roots. In particular, the shop's mixed fruit jelly doughnut is very similar to strawberry jam doughnuts native to Cornwall.

Bill Scantlebury is the third-generation baker-proprietor, a lean, gentle-mannered elderly man who doesn't look as if he ever eats his shop's baked goods. He is so omnipresent that he must sleep on a cot next to the bakery's coal oven. And he practically does—he lives in the apartment above.

Bill's grandfather, William Thomas Scantlebury, came over from England in 1920. "He worked here for two years before sending for his wife and seven children," says Bill. Bill's grandfather learned the bakery business as an apprentice in Cornwall. "He used to take wheat to the mill and tell them how to mill it, then go back and bake the bread, put it on the cart, and go out and sell it." Bill's grandfather bought the East Boston shop, then named Cotty's Bakery, and renamed it Betty Ann after his first grandchild.

The bakery has been handed down from father to son for three generations.

Bill's father, William Ralph Scantlebury, worked in the bakery alongside Bill's grandfather and later became the owner. Bill, too, worked with his father for decades before taking over the reins.

But for the aroma of warm, fresh from the fryer doughnuts, you might just miss them. Set out on two trays behind the counter, they are practically hidden from view.

Bill makes both cake and yeast doughnuts, but offers only five classic types: plain cake, sugared crullers, plain sugar-raised, lemon-filled, and jelly-filled. The cake doughnuts are heavyweights, sugary with a crunchy exterior. The yeast raised doughnuts have a taste of nutmeg and lemon and overflow with filling. The doughnuts are made from scratch every morning from Bill's grandfather's decades-old recipe beginning at 4 a.m. "We don't have any machines and we make everything by hand," says Bill.

Doughnuts are available every day along with a varied selection of delectable baked goods. On weekdays there are Danishes, scones, and cookies. On weekends there are brownies, coffee rolls, and in the ancient bakery case, a proud display of cakes and pies.

On Saturdays, Bill also sells pints of slow-cooked baked beans infused with molasses and a bit of salt pork. Boston may have many nicknames, but locals never refer to the city as "Beantown"; only outsiders do. But the enduring New England tradition of baked beans (usually served with brown bread) for Saturday night supper continues to this day. The custom began with the 17th-century Puritan settlers who would make enough baked beans, kept warm on a banked fire, the night before so they would not have to cook on the Sabbath.

Don't look for a cup of coffee to accompany your doughnut; Bill doesn't want to be bothered with the meal tax. "Once upon a time, coffee and doughnuts were a snack, but now it's a meal. They can't pay me enough to do their bookkeeping," Bill says with a laugh. There's a vintage cash register that tallies amounts only up to $4, so bring cash.

And this is a straight bakery, so there are no seats either. Customers take their brown paper bag of doughnuts to be inhaled in their car or just stand and eat. And yes, the line does form early—on weekends often by 7 a.m.—so you may want to set your alarm. The shop is closed on Monday, is open mornings only, and closes when inventory runs out—sometimes as early as 10 a.m.

The shop enjoys support from a fiercely loyal clientele with deep roots in "Eastie." "There are not only new people, but people who have moved out and come back to visit," says Bill.

Bill may be the last of his family to own the bakery. "I'm not married yet," he jokes. "But I keep going to Britain to visit relatives and see if anyone is interested in coming over." Let's hope someone takes over—Betty Ann's legions of doughnut fans need their sugar high.

BOVA BAKERY

134 SALEM ST. • BOSTON, MA 02113

(617) 523-5601 • BOVABAKERYBOSTON.COM

Open 24/7 for Pastry and Pizza

At the corner of Salem and Prince Streets, in the heart of Italian-American life in Boston, Bova Bakery is an institution. The unmistakable smell of anise wafts through the air the moment you walk in the door. Several display cases show off Bova's enormous—with more than 100 varieties—pastry and cookie selection. How can anybody choose? Among the many tempting treats are flaky, shell-shaped custard-filled *sfogliatelle,* or lobster tails, brightly colored butter cookies, and elegant rum cakes. Bova, though,

is best known for its cannoli, which has a light, crunchy shell and ricotta cream filling that is sweet but not overpoweringly so.

The Bova family has been baking in Boston since 1926, when Antonio and Victoria Bova came from the Calabria region of Italy and opened a small shop in the North End.

By the 1940s three of Antonio's five sons—Ralph, Georgie, and Joseph—had joined the family bakery. Today, the third-generation descendants of Antonio (grandsons and cousins all) share the business: brothers Ralphie and Anthony (sons of Ralph), Dr. Anthony Bova (also the neighborhood dentist) and his brother George (sons of Georgie), and Joey Bova (son of Joseph).

Operating a three-shift, 24-hour bakery can be exhausting. Everything—the bread, pastry and cookies, and pizza and calzone—is made on-site throughout the day. Bova's solution is that each partner family works the bakery for six months and then takes a year off. It's a unique business model.

When the Bova family began the bakery, they only made bread. Bova breads quickly became a mainstay of the neighborhood. "All the old-timers used to have big families that would eat lots of bread. Now the neighborhood is yuppie, uppity," laments Ralphie. In the second generation, Bova still sold bread but also added a delicatessen/

luncheonette. In the 1960s Bova converted back to a bakery-only storefront.

In recent years, bread sales have dropped off and the store has focused more on pastries as well as new ways of bringing in business. The family and the inventory are Italian, but Bova has adapted to new tastes too, introducing s'more brownies and whoopee pies to the menu. Bova has even experimented with online sales. Anthony talks about a recent order of 136 chocolate-dipped cannolis sent to Las Vegas for an Ultimate Fight event. "They paid more for the overnight delivery than for the cannolis," he says, shaking his head.

The sense of Bova family tradition is heightened around the holidays, when the bakery churns out specialties like panettone at Christmas, *zeppole* or custard- and jam-filled cream puffs for St. Joseph's Day in March, and braided bread with dyed hard-boiled eggs at Easter.

Late night in the North End, Bova Bakery is the only place to be. Bova is one of Boston's few 24-hour eateries—and it's open seven days a week. After midnight, a table filled with trays of calzones— chicken Parm, Italian cold cut, spinach, and more, wrapped in wax paper and ready to go—caters to the city's hospital workers, taxicab drivers, tech entrepreneurs, and students.

Much of the Italian bread served in the North End restaurant bread baskets is made here, including crisp baguette-like Bastone and soft, round Tuscan loaves. The breads are from family recipes. "It's just basic stuff: flour, water, salt, and sugar. It's not rocket science," says Anthony.

But when asked about his favorite from the bakery, Anthony doesn't hesitate: "The smell of the hot bread, underneath your arm, walking in the cold. Put on a little butter, oregano, and oil. There's nothing like it."

THE BRATTLE BOOK SHOP

9 WEST ST. • BOSTON, MA 02111

(617) 542-0210 • BRATTLEBOOKSHOP.COM

Serendipitous Book Discoveries

*T*ucked away on an obscure side street near Downtown Crossing, within sight of the State House and just blocks from the Theater District, the Brattle Book Shop is one of the country's oldest sellers of used, out-of-print, and antiquarian books.

Everything from the quaint brick three-story building, to the lovely old-books smell, to the outside sale lot filled with carts of bargain books makes the Brattle Book Shop a literary landmark and a cherished Boston institution.

Established in 1825, the store was named after its first location on Boston's Brattle Street. The shop had changed hands a few times before newlyweds George and Dorrit Gloss bought a half interest in the store in 1949 for $500. Today the store is still family-owned. Ken Gloss inherited the proprietorship of the Brattle Book Shop from his father. Ken recalls," My father built the business with his love of books, his hard work, and his knowledge. He was also somewhat of a character and a showman."

But Ken is legend in his own right, a recognized authority on used and rare books, a frequent guest appraiser on PBS's *Antiques Roadshow,* and a lecturer at libraries and historical societies. Ken grew up among the stacks, working at the Brattle after school and in the summer during college. Between college and grad school Ken returned to the bookshop. "My father's health wasn't that good but quite honestly, I needed a year off. And that was 40 years ago."

In the 60-plus years the Gloss family has owned the store, the Brattle has changed location seven times. It moved into its current premises on West Street in 1969 after the original Brattle Street store was demolished in the name of "urban renewal" to make way for Government Center.

The Brattle is truly a throwback. It's not the place to go for the latest best seller; it's where to go to lose yourself for hours at a time. In an era dominated by online bookstores and e-books, browsing the

shelves of a bookstore is an almost archaic pleasure. It might be the book you've never heard of, located next to the one you are looking for, that is the one you really want or need.

The Brattle stands out among bookstores for its much-loved atmosphere and its crammed but orderly shelves filled with books on every topic imaginable. The first two floors are dedicated to general used books (mostly hard cover and priced in the $5–$10 range) that include literary classics and topics as varied as trolleys, opera, and espionage. Head upstairs to the third floor and you'll find rare first editions, antique maps, and tooled leather volumes to give your living room that library ambience. There is even more to browse in the vacant lot outside—open six days a week—unless it's raining or snowing, with books priced at $1, $3, and $5. Here, you can buy a bag heavy with books for just $10.

New stock arrives constantly; some mornings as many as 4,000 books come in. "If people walk in here two or three times and don't see anything different, then they stop coming," Ken says. He makes house calls several times a week, and works with estates, trust departments, lawyers, auctioneers, and other book dealers. The store also buys from individuals and gives free verbal appraisals. "Today we received a whole series of newspapers from the Civil War. A couple of weeks ago we bought a collection of books on psychoanalysis. And last summer we bought 600 boxes of books on the American West. We just get some very interesting things," he says.

And all sorts of customers scour these shelves for treasured titles, Ken says: "We have students—although students don't have much money. We have street people—some of whom are brilliant. Then there are the people who work in the area who come during their lunch hour. We get tourists and business travelers from all over the country too. And literally, there are a few people who come in just about every single day. There is one guy who calls in when he is sick."

Ken owns the West Street building and its next-door lot. "That's actually what keeps us in business. I like to think that I'm good at bookselling, but if we didn't own the building, we would be priced out of the area."

When asked what's next for the business, Ken isn't sure. His wife, Joyce Kosofsky, works with him, but his two grown daughters are not interested in running the shop. "I love the book business. My intention is to work here as long as I am physically able to do it."

BROMFIELD PEN SHOP

5 BROMFIELD ST. • BOSTON, MA 02108

(617) 482-9053 • BROMFIELDPENSHOP.COM

Still Making Its Mark in a Digital Age

*D*espite a devotion to computers and smart phones, it doesn't take long for even the most casual of browsers at the Bromfield Pen Shop to fall in love with the written word again.

Located at Downtown Crossing, the Bromfield Pen Shop is a modest storefront that gives little indication of the treasures inside.

Especially during the weekday, the little store becomes quite busy with downtown workers who duck in during their lunch hour to check out the stock of fine writing pens (both vintage and new), watches, stylish and modern journals and notebooks by Moleskine and Clairfontaine, Swiss Army knives, and other distinctive gift items.

Bromfield Street itself still has the look and feel of old Boston. The one-way thoroughfare is lined on both sides with mom-and-pop businesses and largely serves as a pedestrian path between the Park Street T station and the office buildings of the financial district.

Ralph Waldo Emerson once remarked of Boston's streets, "We say the cows laid out Boston. Well, there are worse surveyors." Emerson probably knew crooked Bromfield Street well; he was a founding member of the 19th-century Saturday Club, an informal intellectual society that met around the corner at the Parker House Hotel.

Unlike in Emerson's day, the rumble of the T underneath your feet is ever-present in the neighborhood and is particularly noticeable inside the Bromfield Pen Shop. Today the store is owned and operated by Fred Rosenthal, who inherited it from his grandfather, Joe Hamburg. By the 1940s Fred's grandfather had a string of small businesses in the Boston area including a delivery service—which he closed during World War II because no kids were available to do

Vintage Spots: Downtown Crossing

Restaurant Marliave: Est. 1875

Tucked behind an alley and through a courtyard, this Victorian-era town-house restaurant was founded by French immigrant Henry Marliave and is Boston's fourth-oldest restaurant. This one-time speakeasy has recently come back to life; the space retains its modern-vintage feel with a tin ceiling and black and white tiles along with a clutter of dog-eared photos. The restaurant offers a multitude of backdrops: basement oyster bar, main floor cafe, and upstairs fine dining room. Its Prohibition-style libations are done very well; the food leans toward French and American gastropub fare.
10 Bosworth St.; (617) 422-0004; marliave.com

the work—and a wholesale office supply store. "The story is that my grandfather got rid of everything but the pens because he didn't want to haul the paper up and down the steps," says Fred.

The Bromfield Pen Shop has been in its current location since 1948 and has outlasted most of its neighbors—including both Filene's and Jordan Marsh, Boston's homegrown department stores that anchored shopping in this area for generations.

Even with the advent of the office superstores in the 1980s, the Bromfield Pen Shop has managed to survive simply because it is a specialty store selling a niche product. "Our sales have blossomed as pens have become valued as an accessory as much as for their function," explains Fred. "The pen community is a small community. We are the only pen shop in downtown but people know who we are and they find us."

In the early days there were no ballpoint or roller-ball pens, just fountain pens. "Fountain pen people are still our biggest and most regular customers," says Fred. Gleaming limited-edition, collectible fountain pen brands are displayed like jewels in glass cases. Mont Blanc, Waterman, and Parker are coveted by collectors and are the store's biggest sellers. Pen devotees know that fine writing instruments sometimes require maintenance. The Bromfield Pen Shop is also true to the old; the shop's front window is dedicated to the workbench of Bromfield's full-time in-store repairman Greg Byrne, who practices the craft of fixing classic and vintage fountain pens and also does engraving.

There is still something wonderful about writing in longhand. At the gloriously old-fashioned Bromfield Pen Shop you can chat with Fred and try potential pens that are right to hold and right for writing. You won't leave empty-handed.

CAFE ALGIERS

40 BRATTLE ST. • CAMBRIDGE, MA 02138

(617) 492-1557

An Ornately Beautiful Spot That Lets You Sit and Sip Coffee for Hours at a Time

Cafe Algiers embodies the ideal of the Cambridge coffeehouse and is the virtual elder statesman of bohemian Harvard Square hangouts. Forty-plus years ago, when hummus was "exotic" and not available in every run-of-the-mill supermarket, Cafe Algiers was

one of the few places to go in the Boston area for Middle Eastern cuisine.

Palestinian-born owner Emile Durzi opened Cafe Algiers in 1970 inside the subterranean space of Brattle Hall. The Brattle itself has quite a history. The brick barnlike gambrel building dates from 1890 and was originally a live stage and music venue. By the 1950s the space was converted to a first-run cinema and retail space. The Brattle Theater is particularly famous for introducing generations of Harvard students to *Casablanca*. First screened at the Brattle in 1957, the film is shown several times during Valentine's Day week and has a cultlike following among students. Today the Brattle Theater and Cafe Algiers share the space at Brattle Hall. It turns out that the theater's mostly moody art-house movies are a perfect complement to Cafe Algiers' sultry dishes.

Durzi moved Cafe Algiers to the building's larger upstairs space in 1990 and created a darkly atmospheric and romantic setting evocative of a fantasy Kasbah.

The design inspiration is a cross-country hodge-podge drawn from Algeria and Morocco in north Africa, and Turkey and Palestine in the Near East. The focus of the room is the oculus—a circular opening between the first and second floors—and the soaring octagonal wood dome ceiling. The crimson and ochre painted walls are decorated with tiles featuring Arabic calligraphy, intricate silver tooled mirrors, and Moroccan stained-glass lanterns. Latticework archways frame the space, creating quiet nooks offering supreme privacy for young couples and thesis-writing grad students. When the weather is nice, the rooftop outdoor patio is a great little spot to escape the bustle of Harvard Square.

Overall, the ambience encourages low-key lingering. In the Middle East, coffeehouses are traditionally a man's domain where men would while away the hours chatting, reading the daily newspapers, or playing backgammon. Cafe Algiers has several house backgammon boards for patrons' use, and after much lobbying by students, there is free Wi-Fi too. "We have people who spend five or six hours here with one coffee, but we don't bother them," says manager Nadir Bendjenni. Know that if you are in a rush, Cafe Algiers is not your place; the service is purposely slower so that you can enjoy the surroundings and the feeling of the moment.

According to Nadir, the cafe's most popular dishes are its red lentil soup, the house-made lamb mergesa (sausage), and the combination plate of hummus, tabbouleh, lentil pilaf, and baba ghanoush (also all made in-house). Not as well known is that Cafe Algiers is open both early and late—from 8 a.m. to midnight daily. At breakfast it's a place to have a quiet tea with toasted pita, yogurt, and honey. Care for a drink? There's a short list of wine and beer.

But really, you're not coming here for an epic meal—Cafe Algiers is all about sitting at one of the wobbly little tables having strong Turkish coffee served from delicate long-spouted copper ewers and maybe a piece of *besbousa*—a flat syrup-soaked semolina cake— and people-watching the day away. Cafe Algiers has always drawn a mostly intellectual, international crowd of students and a cadre of local characters whose lively communal conversation makes Cafe Algiers a true Cambridge gem.

CAFFE VITTORIA

290–296 HANOVER ST. • BOSTON, MA 02113

(617) 227-7606 • VITTORIACAFFE.COM

It's Not About the Coffee

*C*affe Vittoria is a North End landmark, charming visitors for decades with its elegant space: its tiny marble tables, historic mosaic floor, ornately carved oak bar, and impressive collection of vintage espresso machines.

Opened in 1929, the original Caffe Vittoria was the North End's first cafe. In those days, many of the Italian immigrants in the North End lived in tight quarters and it was here, at places like Caffe Vittoria, that the Italian community came to socialize. It was their home away from home. Eventually Caffe Vittoria closed and over the years the first-floor space was rented out to other businesses: a grocery store, Caffe Paradiso (now down the street), a travel agency, and a bank. At one time, the basement space housed an Italian restaurant, Grotta Azura, an Italian restaurant that the famed Italian-born tenor Enrico Caruso used to frequent when he was performing in Boston.

For nearly 100 years, the six-story late 1800s building has been owned by three generations of the North End's Riccio family. In 1980 Gerry Riccio, just 22 at the time, bought the building from his family. "I was a licensed plumber. I wasn't good at school, but I was good at working," says Gerry. Gerry's wife, Linda, puts it another way: "Gerry has a natural ability to build businesses."

Soon after acquiring the Hanover Street property, the Riccios decided to reopen Caffe Vittoria. Gerry sees his role as helping to preserve the neighborhood. "We wanted to keep the name Caffe Vittoria because it had a history here in the neighborhood," says Linda. The Riccios now own three other businesses in the neighborhood:

Stanza dei Sigari (a cigar bar in the basement space of Caffe Vit-toria), Florentine Cafe (farther down Hanover Street), and the fine dining restaurant Gennaro's 5 North Square, located a few doors from the Paul Revere House. Says Gerry, "We were the youngest business-people in the North End and now we are the oldest."

For the Riccios, business is thriving. Linda attributes their success to their location in the North End and her and Gerry's passion for making it work. Linda adds, "And a great product. Not a good prod-uct, but a great product. You want to give people what you would like yourself."

Caffe Vittoria is almost always open, from first coffee at sunrise until late nightcap in the evening (or early morning). In the morn-ing it's an ideal spot for breakfast and the newspaper (or quiet con-templation). At mid-afternoon it is still peaceful enough that you can enjoy a good conversation. In the evening the older, larger section of the cafe is opened. It's always busy, but you'll never feel rushed out, because there is ample seating and there is always room for

newcomers. Caffe Vittoria also has three full liquor bars. As the day turns to night, regulars stop by for an *apertivo* like a Campari spritzer or a glass of *prosecco* before dinner—after dinner for a *digestivo* of grappa or *vin santo*. Around midnight the cafe attracts groups of hungry college revelers for coffee, Italian pastries like cannoli and tiramisu, gelati, and lots of late-night talking.

No matter the time of day or night, the people-watching at Caffe Vittoria is always first-rate, as are the strong coffee drinks—cappuccinos are what crowds the tables most. And like many North End establishments, Caffe Vittoria is cash only.

The carefully crafted coffee making and Italian pastries are beside the point here: It's Caffe Vittoria's Old World atmosphere that is the true draw for tourists and residents.

CARDULLO'S

6 BRATTLE ST. • CAMBRIDGE, MA 02138

(617) 491-8888 • CARDULLOS.COM

All the Ingredients for Success

Jn Cambridge, all roads lead to Harvard Square. Located at this most celebrated of crossroads is Cardullo's, which upon opening in 1950 perfected, if not pioneered, the idea of gourmet food shopping in the Boston area.

Born in Messina, Italy, in 1915, Frank Cardullo immigrated with his family to the US when he was 4 years old. Cardullo came to the Square in 1943 when he bought Cambridge's historic Wursthaus restaurant, which he ran until it closed in 1993. He leased a storefront across the street and established Cardullo's in 1950.

"We say in the family that Grandfather opened up Cardullo's so that my grandmother would have something to do," says Donez Cardullo, who co-owns the store with her sister Francesca. Their brother Marc pitches in during the weekends.

What was originally conceived as a small delicatessen has grown over the years to encompass a specialty food store. "As air travel became more common in the 1950s my grandparents traveled quite a bit and discovered all these marvelous things: mustards from France and truffles from Italy. One thing led to another and now we have more than 3,000 items from around the world," says Donez.

Donez's father, also named Frank Cardullo, took over Cardullo's in 1988. "This store was his passion," remembers Donez. "I have a degree in psychology, which is important in this business, especially in Harvard Square, but my real experience is working from the ground up with my dad for 10 years."

Home to Harvard University, Cambridge has always attracted a well-educated and well-traveled clientele as well as an international crowd. Cramped and convivial, the layout of the narrow shop encourages browsing. The inventory is fascinating and prices are a little dear, but for sophisticates and ex-pats, Cardullo's is well worth a visit.

Reflecting the Cardullo family heritage, the canned and prepared sections lean toward Italian, with lots of sauces, pasta, and antipasti. Cardullo's claim to fame may just be its chocolate wall, with everything from Belgian Neuhaus truffles to Kit Kat bars from England, and original Nutella in glass jars imported from Italy. Beer, wine, and champagne were added in the 1970s. "We have a tremendous craft beer selection, probably the best in the Square," says Donez. And Cardullo's artfully assembled gift baskets are chock-full of high-quality goods.

But aside from hard-to-find gourmet and specialty foods, what sets Cardullo's apart from the competition is its selection of fresh-made sandwiches that feature artisan cheese and charcuterie. The current roster of sandwiches includes a very popular upscale Italian

sub and the Catherine the Great: Osetra caviar and crème fraîche on a baguette that costs $100. Donez says that they sell anywhere from one to three caviar sandwiches a year, "often when a professor gets tenure."

Moving forward, Cardullo's has diversified its product mix to include more local foods. "Until recently, Cardullo's has always been about imports, imports, imports," says Donez. "But there are some really fabulous items available from around the corner too, so we have made it our mission to feature great local New England products like Harbor Sweets Chocolates, Effie's Oatcakes, and Q's nuts.

The Cardullo family has been in Harvard Square for more than 70 years and in 1996, the corner of Brattle and JFK Streets was named Frank Cardullo Square to honor the family patriarch. Today Cardullo's remains one of Cambridge's best-loved businesses as the third-generation Cardullo legacy continues to contribute in making Harvard Square a vibrant community, and a place where people want to come to shop and visit.

CHARLES STREET SUPPLY

54–56 CHARLES ST. • BOSTON, MA 02114

(617) 367-9046 • CHARLESSTSUPPLY.COM

A Hardware Store
as Urban Resource Center

*I*n 1948, Ralph Block opened a hardware store, Charles Street Supply, in the basement of 89 Charles St. It was a general hardware store that catered to Boston's historic Beacon Hill, which has always included a large number of high-maintenance federal-style townhomes.

Ralph, however, was known in the neighborhood as a somewhat grumpy and surly shopkeeper. During that time period, Dick Gurnon worked as a hardware jobber, who often called on Ralph in the course of his business supplying hardware stores with merchandise. By 1952, Dick had convinced Ralph to take him on as a partner; Ralph was in charge of the back office work, while Dick was the front man. Between the two of them, the store did very well. By 1958, the store had moved to bigger quarters at 43 Charles St. and by 1960, Dick had bought out Ralph. However, in 1963 a fire in the back alley destroyed the store, forcing Dick to relocate and buy the building of its current home at 54–56 Charles St. "We really had nothing left to sell other than some paint, a few pieces of Pyrex, and some cleaning supplies," recalls Dick's son, Jack Gurgon. "Now we have nearly 40,000 SKU's." The building itself has an interesting history: It was once a fine furniture factory, then a fish market and a Chinese laundry.

Jack is fond of saying he has worked at Charles Street Supply "as long as I could look over the counter and make change." Jack came to work full-time in 1977, after graduating from UMass, eventually taking over the reins of the business from his father. Jack lives in the

apartment over the store, with his wife and two teenage daughters. "Beacon Hill is almost like a village. We all really do know each other here."

It's easy to forget amid the astonishing assortment of house wares (coffeemakers and vacuum cleaners) and general merchandise (aspirin, jars of pickles, baseballs, and notebook paper) that the traditional nuts-and-bolts hardware stock here is as good as any in the city. Yes, you can get a lot of these things elsewhere, but Jack and his staff can concisely tell you how to unclog a drain or how to go about painting a room or refer you to a local handyman if the job is too big for DIY.

The basement holds the more heavy-duty stuff: cut-to-order lumber, window screens, and the store's ever-popular key cutting service (a lot of college students live in the neighborhood too). The store's most popular items are lightbulbs, cleaning supplies, and mousetraps. "It's the city," Jack says with a laugh. He adds, "I've also been told by my supplier that we sell more silver polish than any other hardware store in New England." Because of its Beacon Hill location, Charles

Street Supply gets a lot of international tourists as well, who tend to favor made-in-America goods like Maglites, Leatherman multi-tools, and Weber grills.

What's the future of the business? Jack is enthusiastic. "I love what I do. Every day is different. I am a hero to someone every single day. But can I see my daughters doing it? No. It's a lot of hours for not a lot of money. Charles Street Supply is something that the neighborhood needs. It's something that every single neighborhood should have. Unfortunately, we don't anymore. But the nice thing about Beacon Hill is that people get it. They know if you don't shop at their local stores, they are not going to be here anymore."

CHEAPO RECORDS

538 MASSACHUSETTS AVE. • CAMBRIDGE, MA 02139
(617) 354-4455 • CHEAPORECORDS.COM

A Boston-Area Musical Mainstay

€ven in the era of iTunes, this neighborhood record store carries on. Located in Central Square, one of Greater Boston's most eclectic neighborhoods, this old-school record store draws collectors and bargain hunters alike. The nice, non-stereotypical record store clerks are helpful and know just about everything there is about

music. And as you would expect for a place with "Cheapo" as part of the name, prices here are really low.

The store focuses mainly on used vinyl, and the selection is unmatched in the Boston area: classic, jazz, independents, and imports. There's no crate-digging here; Cheapo is open and brightly lit, and the packed record bins are highly organized by genre, sub-genre, and often down to the artist. The store truly stocks every kind of music imaginable from every decade; you'll find Hank Williams, John Coltrane, Barry Manilow, Japanese punk, the odd musical soundtrack, labels of the current Boston music scene, and lots of unclassifiables. The store also features a sizeable used and new CD collection and even some cassettes, along with 78s and 45s.

Everybody in the Boston music world knows Cheapo Records, which was founded by Sid Rivco in 1948 and began as the Cambridge Music Box on Prospect Street. The store moved to 645 Massachusetts Ave. in 1954 before ending up at its current storefront 2 blocks down the street in 2005. Its location around the corner from Central Square's venerable live music club, the Middle East, is notable too as the store has always been a gathering place for working musicians and other music enthusiasts.

Current owner Allen Day, an avid record collector himself, bought the store in 1975 not long after serving in Vietnam. "At the time, I owned a business called Cheapo Movers, which I gave up to take on the record store. I renamed the store Cheapo Records with the idea of selling all cut-outs or discontinued records. Various old-timers taught me the business, and I traveled around the country buying inventory."

Today the vast majority of Cheapo's stock comes through the front door. According to Allen, record retailing is a business of friends. Allen says, "We are painfully careful not to buy things that are a problem and we stand behind what we sell."

Allen remembers the 1950s through the 1970s, before the demise of rent control, when Central Square was a working-class neighborhood, "when working class meant that people had some money to spend. There were jobs at the shoe factory and the bakery and people bought music."

Not everyone has been converted by the clean sound of CDs. All these years later, some of the people who buy at Cheapo are old-timers looking to buy a Platters or a Jimi Hendrix LP. Allen says, "It is commonly believed that more and more people are buying records. More young people are becoming interested in analog sound and vinyl." And a good number of Allen's customers are collectors. He calls them "pre-responsibility yuppies," mostly guys ages 18 to 40 that have some disposable income and have decided to collect records.

According to Allen, business is looking up. "I hope that the Cheapo will be around for a while. I can't say that it will be forever, but as long as I have someone interested in operating it, the store will remain."

CHINA PEARL

9 TYLER ST. • BOSTON, MA 02111

(617) 426-4338 • CHINAPEARLBOSTON.COM

Dim Sum Grandeur

Bustling and noisy, Boston's historic Chinatown is shoehorned between Downtown Crossing and the South End. Immigrant Chinese workers first arrived in Boston in the 1870s, settling in the vicinity of Kneeland, Beach, and Tyler Streets. Back then, Chinese workers easily found work in the garment factories and leather tanneries adjacent to nearby South Station.

Over the years the neighborhood has seen successive waves of Chinese immigrants. And although hardly 1 square mile, today Boston's Chinatown is the third largest in the country. Over time, gentrification has wiped out the factories that once dominated the neighborhood. In their stead, Chinatown's former factory buildings are now luxury condos that cater to young professionals. But the labyrinth of streets is still alive day and night, home to restaurants, bakeries, and grocery stores, and is still one of Boston's most flourishing ethnic neighborhoods.

Boston has a long lineage of Chinese restaurants—none more esteemed than Chinatown's oldest restaurant, China Pearl. This 745-seat old-school dim sum parlor is a steadfastly excellent Chinatown restaurant.

Change doesn't come easily in Chinatown, though. The space is boldly decorated in Hong Kong style with plum trees, red lanterns, and golden dragons that wrap around the perimeter of the dining room. A la carte dim sum is offered every day from 8:30 a.m. to 9:30 p.m. And during dim sum prime time—on Saturday and Sunday from 11 a.m. to 3 p.m.—a long line snakes down the stairs and out the door. Best to just embrace the chaos of a gang of waitresses pushing roving trolleys stacked with plates of superlative dumplings and pillowy soup buns along with deep-fried chicken feet—if you dare.

China Pearl was opened in 1963 by brothers Frank and Bill Chin, still considered Chinatown's godfathers—and referred to as Uncle Frank and Uncle Bill in the neighborhood. Back in the '70s, Uncle Frank also worked as a purchaser for the City of Boston. He was able to deliver the Chinese vote to the Democrats in exchange for improvements in the Chinatown community.

China Pearl continues to wield influence in the neighborhood. Ever since the Moy family bought China Pearl from the Chin family in 1988, the family has been a force in Chinatown. Ricky Moy arrived in Boston in 1964 from his native Hong Kong at the age of 16 with next to nothing. His first job was working as a bus boy at China Pearl. Throughout the '70s and '80s Ricky established several businesses of his own: bakeries, barbecue shops, and restaurants in Chinatown.

Today Ricky's children, Brian and Patricia Moy, are the brother-and-sister pair who runs China Pearl. American-born and raised in nearby Milton, the Moy siblings are both young and highly educated

(Brian graduated from Boston University, Patricia from Boston University and Boston College) and represent a new breed of Chinese restaurant entrepreneurs. "We know that the community is changing and we want to change along with it," says Brian. Chinatown used to be mainly immigrant families. Now there are fewer families and more young professionals and students from Tufts Medical Center. It's a fine line for China Pearl, which acts as a de facto community center to lifelong Chinatown residents and also caters to "ABCs" (American-born Chinese) as well as tourists. "Our quality and service standards are becoming higher," says Brian. Patricia adds, "Before it was accepted that our staff didn't have to speak English. Now we have two levels of English classes taught on-site two times a week."

The Moys' latest expansion embodies this change. Shojo, located below China Pearl, is part pub, part trendy Asian eatery. Shojo offers pan-Asian small plates like fluffy pork belly *bao* (buns) with salted daikon and cucumber and duck tacos with kimchee slaw along with playful drinks like a scorpion jar for two. In conjunction with the city, the Moys have also recently embarked on a green renovation project at China Pearl incorporating recycled materials and clean energy production.

Patricia says that despite recent changes, China Pearl is still community based. "On weekdays, we see a lot of the regulars that have been coming every day for 10 to 20 years. They bring their newspaper up. They may only eat one or two things and spend a couple of hours mingling with friends. When they don't come, we get worried.

"A lot of the things that we do are not about making money; it's about giving back to the community for all the support that they have given our family over the years."

CLUB PASSIM

47 PALMER ST. • CAMBRIDGE, MA 02138

(617) 492-7679 • PASSIM.ORG

A Slice of Folk History

One of the country's most legendary folk haunts, Harvard Square's Club Passim has introduced dozens of greats on their way up. The roster of folk and blues luminaries who first found their voice here begins with Bonnie Raitt, Joan Baez, Peter Wolf, and Joni Mitchell and extends through today's biggest names like Suzanne Vega, Ellis Paul, and Maeve Gilchrist.

Club Passim has a huge reputation as the epicenter of Boston's folk scene, but the 102-seat underground venue itself is really very small. The room is scruffy and dark, with a cramped stage. An always-busy vegetarian restaurant (this is Cambridge, after all) shares the space too. Club Passim draws a devoted, knowledgeable folkie crowd that appreciates songs and songwriting. A good many of the patrons are friends of the musicians, so it's the kind of place where the audience and performers mingle between sets. It's a great listening room.

In the 1950s and '60s Cambridge was an integral part of the American folk music revival. Disillusioned with rock music and drawn to the simple tunes and meaningful lyrics by singer-songwriters like Woody Guthrie and Pete Seeger, Boston-area college students and young musicians gathered at coffeehouses, bars, and record stores in Cambridge and created a musical community. Club Passim started out in 1958 as Club 47, a jazz coffeehouse opened by Paula Kelley and Joyce Kalina and was named after its address, 47 Mount Auburn St. It soon changed to an all-folk format and became the place for folk musicians to play and hang out. In its heyday in the 1960s,

Cambridge's burgeoning folk scene was closely associated with both the civil rights and Vietnam anti-war movements. Club 47 moved to its current alleyway location on Palmer Street in 1963, but financial difficulties forced its doors closed in 1968.

In 1969 Bob and Rae Anne Donlin took over the Club 47 space with the intention of running a card and gift shop. Folk fans and musicians would often stop by and ask, "Where's the music?" So the Donlins became almost accidental keepers of the folk movement, returning the club to its folk music coffeehouse roots and booking talent for the next 25 years. They renamed the space Passim—pronounced "Pass-eem," which is Latin for a "footnote occurring here and there within a text"; the literary reference reflects the club's many functions.

When the Donlins retired in 1994, Passim closed down with a six-figure debt. Renamed Club Passim and incorporated as a nonprofit in 1995, today the club presents nearly 400 shows a year and is noted for its school of music and community outreach programming. Matt Smith has been Club Passim's managing director and booking agent since 2008—and a Passim fan since the early 1990s. He describes Club Passim's line-up as mostly a mix of regional and local folk acts. Other programming highlights include its Campfire Festivals that take place over the Memorial Day and Labor Day weekends and frequent open-mic nights throughout the year. Notably no longer alcohol-free, Club Passim has been serving beer and wine at shows since 2009.

"We also sponsor a monthly series with Berklee's American Roots Program which gives student musicians an opportunity to try out their music and get noticed," says Smith. And folk headliners are still known to drop in at Club Passim when they are in town: "They got their start here and remember when no one would listen to them; they always like to come back. It a small community," he says.

DEVENEY & WHITE

664 GALLIVAN BLVD. • BOSTON, MA 02124
(617) 288-3080 • DEVENEYANDWHITE.COM

Carved in Stone—Creating Works of Lasting Beauty

A slight young woman, Elizabeth Deveney Frazier is not the typical image of an owner of a memorial business that specializes in headstones. Describing a recent engraving project for Liberty Mutual's corporate offices, she says, "It came out awesome."

Elizabeth is the fourth-generation owner of Deveney & White. "We have a lot of pride in our small family business." Elizabeth's great-great-grandfather came over to America from County Cork, Ireland, in the late 1800s and initially found work as a shoemaker at Faneuil Hall. He settled in Quincy, which at the time had developed a granite industry—dozens of quarries had opened to supply the American building boom of the late 19th century. By 1898 Elizabeth's great-grandfather, Edward P. Deveney, along with his six younger brothers, had established Deveney Brothers Wholesale Granite, which excavated and shipped granite throughout New England.

In 1946, Edward P. Deveney and his son Edward P. Deveney Jr. (Elizabeth's grandfather) established the family's retail location. Elizabeth describes the company's first building as little more than a "chicken coop" with a backyard work shed on what was then a rural stretch of Dorchester's Gallivan Boulevard. By 1949 a more permanent showroom had been built on the property. During that time and through the 1960s, Elizabeth's great-uncle Mike did all the company's stonecutting and sandblasting work. Great-uncle Mike's

image—wearing work clothes and suspenders, chisel and hammer in hand—is memorialized today in the company's logo.

By the late 1970s, Elizabeth's father, Gerry Deveney, and his brother-in-law Walter White purchased the business, establishing Deveney & White. Elizabeth's brother, Matthew, joined his father in the early '90s. Matthew had grown up setting stones and helping Gerry in the shop—drafting, sandblasting, and sales. It was the only job he ever had. When Matthew passed away in 2007 from cancer at the age of 35, Elizabeth decided to help out the family temporarily.

"I had worked in the music, real estate, and advertising fields. Coming from the corporate world, I have to say that running a small family business is totally different. But I feel so much better." Elizabeth, married and the mother of three young children, now manages the business full-time. Her parents, Gerry and Missy, still help out part-time.

There is an art to stonecutting, but the monument business also requires compassion and sensitivity. Says Elizabeth, "I came into the business after a huge loss of our own, so I can completely relate to how our customers are feeling. But we try not to be focused on the sadness, but on the positive, creating a beautiful memorial for their loved one. "

Elizabeth usually has customers pick their color first. Deveney & White offers rare and lovely stones from all over the world: soft gray from Vermont, royal green from Nova Scotia, black from China, and a

Vintage Spot: Mattapan
SIMCO'S AT THE BRIDGE: EST. 1935

Under a great 1930s-era sign, this is one of the last surviving workingman take-out stands in the city. The best thing on the menu is the simplest: the juicy, chili-topped foot-long hot dog served on a buttered, grilled roll. Popular with the city's taxicab drivers, Simco's busiest time is actually on Sunday, when much of the Baptist congregation across the street comes for hot dogs wearing their Sunday best.
1509 Blue Hill Ave.; (617) 296-3800

rich mahogany from North Dakota. As for designs, Deveney & White has done everything from very simple markers to elaborate freestanding sculpted memorials. A full-size hand-drawn draft is created for each customer. Elizabeth says, "We find if it is drawn by hand and sandblasted by hand, it comes out a lot better, and long-term, people are a lot more satisfied." Deveney & White uses Old World techniques for cutting the stone along with sandblasting and etching to create distinctive, beautifully crafted memorials that are works of art.

Deveney & White doesn't just make headstones; the company has also received commissions for civic memorials and public art installations throughout the area. Among the Deveney & White projects that visitors to Boston may come across are the Charlestown Firefighter Memorial, the engraving for the Harriet Tubman Memorial in the South End, and along the waterfront, the Massachusetts Beirut Memorial at Christopher Columbus Park.

Elizabeth says, "I really, truly feel that I am carrying on a family legacy. It's always a part of the conversation with customers. I'm so proud to say that this is my great-great-grandfather's business that has been passed down within our family through the generations."

DOYLE'S CAFE

3484 WASHINGTON ST. • BOSTON, MA 02130

(617) 524-2345 • DOYLESCAFEBOSTON.COM

Where Irish-American Locals and Tourists Rub Shoulders Over Sam Adams Beer

You enter a time warp when you come to Doyle's, a Boston landmark in the city's Jamaica Plain neighborhood that has been in business since 1882, including a Prohibition-era stint as a suspiciously popular candy store.

Aesthetically, Doyle's is a cross between a traditional Irish pub and a museum of Boston political history. Murals, faded black and white photos of Boston politicians, and Irish signage adorn practically every inch of the walls. The decor also includes an early 1900s wood telephone that was in heavy use in the days when the bar used to get incoming calls for the guys at the bar betting on baseball, boxing, and horses.

In the front, there's a large snug to hide away in, just beside the entrance. The pub's original, lovingly worn wood booths are here too, while the back rooms tend to fill up with local families and tourists who come for the terrific burgers and famous clam chowder, which are the highlights of the menu. The "best seats" in the house, though, are at the 48-foot-long gleaming mahogany bar where the friendly bartenders are happy to pull you a pint from among the impressive selection of 22 taps.

Third-generation owner Gerry Burke Sr.'s stories tumble forth easily as he describes his family's legacy. During the turn of the last century, his grandfather William J. Burke came over from Galway and settled in Boston. "In those days you went to your local saloon to find opportunities to work," he says. "My grandfather happened to wander into Doyle's and became friendly with the owners. During Prohibition, Doyle's operated as a speakeasy and my grandfather opened Burke's Candy Store in this same building, which was really a front for a gin mill for Doyle's." By 1928, with the help of legendary four-time Boston mayor James Michael Curley, the Burke family ran the refreshment concessions at nearby Franklin Park. Gerry, along with his brothers Billy and Eddie, bought the bar from the Doyle family in 1971. "Back then this was a tough neighborhood, but we took a shot at it."

"Growing up in this city, I have never seen those streets look so clean as they do today. There was an awful period in the '70s and '80s, but now business is much better," he says. These days Gerry Sr. comes in only on Friday and Saturday, the bar's busiest days, warmly welcoming both old friends and newcomers. "My son Gerry Jr. runs Doyle's with his partner Chris Spellman. Chris Spellman's father and I grew up together—he's my godson—our families are very close."

Doyle's is located less than a mile from the Sam Adams Brewery, and the bar and the beer company enjoy a special relationship. "One day in 1985, I was working behind the bar and a young Jim Koch comes in with a new brew." Burke is proud to say, "We were the first bar to carry Sam Adams Boston Lager." Sam Adams offers

special-release beers seasonally, and even today Doyle's frequently gets the first kegs.

Over the years legions of politicians, both local and national, have stopped in for a drink. To this day, President John F. Kennedy lingers long in the memory of many Doyle's customers. Senator Ted Kennedy dedicated the John F. "Honey Fitz" Fitzgerald room in 1988 in honor of his maternal grandfather, the former mayor of Boston—and his brother President Kennedy's namesake. "I wouldn't change it for the world," says Gerry Sr. "I still can't talk about John Kennedy without getting tears in my eyes. As an Irish kid, I was so proud when he became president."

Says Gerry Sr., "We want customers to come back. It's nothing fancy, but we offer good food and drink at a good price and personable service. We want our customers to walk out of here happy."

DURGIN PARK

NORTH MARKET BUILDING, FANEUIL HALL • BOSTON, MA 02109

(617) 227-2038 • ARKRESTAURANTS.COM/DURGIN_PARK.HTML

A Dining Room Preserved in Amber

*U*p the dark, old staircase, to a boisterous dining room ruled by no-nonsense waitresses, customers who ask, "Can I have some water?" may get the answer, "The only way you are getting any water is if you pour it yourself or pray for rain."

A good story always comes from dining at Durgin Park. As odd as it may seem, patrons come as much for Durgin Park's famously sharp-tongued (yet deep-down, totally lovable) waitresses as they do for the Indian pudding (made from cornmeal, molasses, and brown sugar) and Boston baked beans.

A Boston institution for almost 200 years, Durgin Park has more than its fair share of character. Generations of customers have been dining on hearty Yankee classics like fish cakes, chicken potpie, and corn bread in a dining room that seems preserved in time; many on the waitstaff have been working at Durgin Park for generations, too.

The mood is captured by sepia-toned photographs that hang on the wall featuring diners from the 1940s dressed in their Sunday best, seated on bentwood chairs, at tables covered in red and white checked tablecloths. Today Durgin Park's dining rooms remains delightfully old-fashioned—with the same tin ceiling and brass coatracks, the same checked tablecloths, and the same small, wobbly chairs.

Customers appreciate the comfortable, unchanging quality of dining at Durgin Park. Gina Schertzer, who has been working as a waitress here since 1975, says, "When people walk up the stairs, they become so excited, remembering visiting here 30 or 40 years ago. People know that this is one place where they can close their eyes and still taste the same chowder, the same Indian pudding, and the same broth in the pot roast. Maybe not on a daily basis, just once in a while. That's what this place is all about."

Located in one of the oldest parts of the city, in an area that in colonial times was Boston's waterfront and working market, Durgin Park has operated continuously for nearly two centuries. It has survived the political, social, and economic upheaval of the Civil War, Prohibition, the Depression, and two world wars. Through it all, "Durgin Park never lost its pizzazz," says Gina.

It's remarkable, too, that Durgin Park has changed hands only four times. Nearby Faneuil Hall and the adjacent Quincy Market were the first wholesale food warehouses in Boston and have operated here, in one form or other, since 1742. Durgin Park was founded by butchers John Durgin and Eldridge Park in 1827 as a no-frills dining room that catered to the lunch trade of fishermen, longshoremen, and out-of-town farmers who worked in the market stalls, by offering a quick meal at communal dining tables for next to nothing. By 1840, Durgin and Park had taken on a third partner, John Chandler, who along with his family owned the restaurant for nearly 100 years,

changing Durgin Park from a working-class lunchroom to a bustling, full-fledged restaurant.

In the years after World War II, the Hallet family became the proprietors and are most remembered by locals for putting Edgar Guest's poem "Just a Boy" on the back of the menu (where it remains to this day) as a tribute to their son who died in the Vietnam War. Then, in 1972 the Kelley family bought the restaurant just as the area was being transformed by Mayor Kevin White's program of urban renewal from a gritty, run-down skid-row neighborhood into Faneuil Hall Marketplace, one of the nation's first festival marketplaces.

Today, if communal tables are new, fresh, and trendy, then Durgin Park's station 12 is legendary. According to Gina, during the restaurant's heyday in the 1970s, the long table in the front dining room was full every day at lunch with single customers drinking manhattans with their steaks and broiled fish. These days, most of the dining room's seating consists of standard four-tops with just four communal tables to carry on the Durgin Park tradition—and to cater to large bus group reservations.

The Ark restaurant group bought Durgin Park from the Kelley family in 2007, but few changes have made their way onto the menu. While the food won't win any awards, you won't be disappointed with traditional favorites like chicken livers in wine, baked scrod, corned beef with cabbage, and apple pan dowdy. You won't leave hungry either, as the portions are huge. According to Gina, the baked beans have actually been improved over the years—"they've added some spice to the original recipe"—and the menu now includes pasta, which was "just" introduced in the 1990s to appeal to customers running the Boston Marathon.

To be sure, there are fewer older steady customers at Durgin Park. Yet, crowds of out-of-towners come year after year, decade after decade, drawn more than anything by the opportunity to experience a Boston original and solid, traditional New England cuisine.

E.B. HORN

429 WASHINGTON ST. • BOSTON, MA 02108

(617) 542-3902 • EBHORN.COM

Flawlessly Standing the Test of Time

*I*t is not uncommon for E.B. Horn to have customers bring in a watch for repair that was purchased at the store by an ancestor more than a century ago. Edwin Booth Horn, a tinkerer and amateur inventor, founded E.B. Horn, one of today's oldest family-run and family-owned jewelry stores in the country.

By 1839 Horn was working as a machinist for the electromagnetic instrument shop of Daniel Davis on Cornhill Street in the area of present-day Boston City Hall Plaza. By 1848, Horn had struck out on his own, opening a watch, clock, and jewelry store on Hanover Street in the city's North End neighborhood.

After Horn's death in 1872, his son Edwin B. Horn Jr. inherited the business and in 1878, he traded up, moving the store to its current site on Washington Street at Downtown Crossing. Located in an 1848 granite Greek Revival building—one of the few surviving structures of the Great Boston Fire of 1872—the new store incorporated elegant hand-crafted wood and glass display cases, a grand brass chandelier, and a rare six-foot-tall 1839 astronomical regulator clock—charming features that remain and embellish the store today.

Benjamin Finn purchased Edwin B. Horn in 1947. The store was about to be liquidated, but Finn saw its potential. E.B. Horn's current co-owners are two of his grandsons (cousins) who have painstakingly built the company to become the jeweler of choice among Boston brides—or perhaps more exactly, their grooms. E.B. Horn's main business is, and has always been, diamonds, offering an array of timeless engagement rings and glittering wedding bands. Luxury timepieces

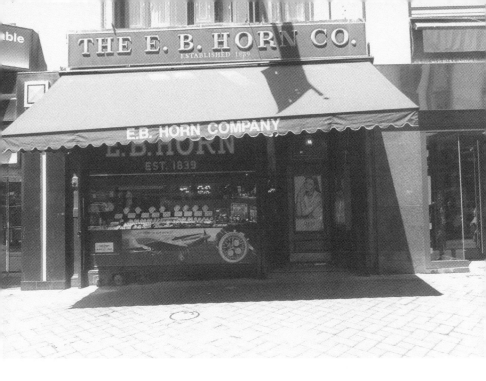

are another focus (Breitling and Tissot), as is its special-occasion collection of sparklers from, among others, Charles Krypell and Norman Covan. E.B. Horn is also the biggest buyer and seller of estate jewelry in the city, so don't be surprised to see vintage Tiffany or Cartier among its baubles and gems.

E.B. Horn especially shines when it comes to service, encouraging questions and try-ons, while developing relationships with its customers who come in year after year, generation after generation. And the collective knowledge of the staff extends way beyond the 4 C's of diamonds. The average length of employment of the staff is in excess of 20 years; the longest-tenured employee has been at E.B. Horn for nearly 50 years.

Robbery stories? Like any jewelry store, E.B. Horn is not immune to break-ins. One of the more memorable burglaries occurred more than 50 years ago, when professional thieves lowered themselves on ropes from the next-door building *Topkapi* style, coming into the store through the skylight. The villains fled with some inventory but were unable to get into any of the store's safes.

During the second half of the 19th century, E.B. Horn, along with New England's renowned homegrown department stores—Filene's,

Jordan Marsh, and Gilchrist's—helped to establish Washington Street as Boston's preeminent shopping district. By the early part of the 20th century the department stores had vanished—victims of changing times and rampant real estate development. Yet, E.B. Horn has stood its ground here for nearly 180 years. And if that doesn't mean it is doing something right, nothing does.

FRANK'S STEAKHOUSE

2310 MASSACHUSETTS AVE. • CAMBRIDGE, MA 02140

(617) 661-0666 • FRANKSSTEAKHOUSE.COM

Calling All Carnivores

This place has been around since the Great Depression and still operates much as it did when Bill Ravinis Sr. bought it in 1974.

Opened in 1938 by local all-around good guy Red O'Connell, Frank's was originally located across the street and is said to be the Boston area's oldest steak house. But who is Frank? According to Bill's son, current owner George Ravinis, it's unclear. Some say a "Frank Viano" at one time owned the land; others say "Frank" was a resident regular at the bar. What is known is that today there is no Frank, but the name remains.

Frank's moved to its current Mass Avenue location in 1940. According to George, Red knew how to run a bar. He also had a cook, Wee Leo, who was well known for his ability to cook steak and chops—and if you asked for it, Chinese food (chop suey was considered exotic back then).

From the seating design, to the faithful waitresses, to the cocktail lounge, most things haven't changed here for decades—and that's a good thing. Frank's is the kind of neighborhood restaurant that attracts a mixed crowd: Cambridge professors and professionals, city workers, retirees, and everyday families. There aren't a lot of culinary bells and whistles on this menu. What you will find is a steak house that offers a lot of value to its customers; the portions are large and the prices are more than fair. Frank's signature 16-ounce strip sirloin is delivered sizzling and well charred with two sides, and at half the price you would find in Boston.

"It must be in the Greek blood to own a restaurant," jokes George, who co-owns Frank's with his brother Bill. "My old man was a businessman, not a restaurateur." Born in Cambridge, Bill Sr. worked for Table Top Pies and dabbled in real estate. Bill then bought a dive bar called The Oaks in nearby Inman Square and later the Cafe in Kendall Square. George says, "My dad bought this, then sold that. He took a shot. Each place was bigger than the other."

After graduating from Boston College, George played some minor league baseball.

But he has worked in the family businesses since he was a teenager. "Being a family business, I was hired and fired a number of times," he says with a laugh.

At one time North Cambridge was a close-knit Irish community, known as "Old Dublin." This was also the home turf of legendary Massachusetts politician Thomas "Tip" O'Neill who served 40 years as a member of the US Congress and 10 years as Speaker of the House of Representatives. "In the old days, all the local pols would be in the bar and Tip would be king of all of them," recalls George. Always popular with people from Cambridge, Frank's now draws an affluent crowd from neighboring towns like Arlington, Winchester, and Lexington. Frank's menu has changed to reflect the market. George says, "We try to keep up with trends. We just put a bacon mac and cheese on the menu. Ten years ago we would have said that mac and cheese was too old-fashioned." He explains further, "Our original wine list had a burgundy, a Chablis, and the pink one. Now our wine list is handpicked to offer several solid, medium-priced wines to our customers." And the chicken souvlaki is a nod to the Ravinis family's Greek heritage.

According to George, the smoking ban killed Frank's late-night bar business.

And although business is coming back, it may never be like the old days. "What's different now is that we have to work harder for every customer that comes through the door."

GALLERIA UMBERTO

289 HANOVER ST. • BOSTON, MA 02113

(617) 227-5709

Cheap and Delicious Italian Street Food in the North End

Slabs of Sicilian pizza and overstuffed calzones accompanied by house wine served in a paper cup are still the best reasons to trek to this been-around-forever North End hole-in-the-wall. But you may want to check your pretensions at the door.

Galleria Umberto is one of those places with an abundance of character—it's an old-school cafeteria-style pizza joint where you order at the counter, pay, wait for your food, and take your tray to the dining room.

The seating area is nothing to speak of—the room is dominated by a full-wall mural map of Italy and features wood-grain Formica tables and standard issue metal restaurant-supply chairs. Here you'll find suits from Government Center side-by-side with tourists, workers from the Charlestown Coast Guard station, and families from the neighborhood.

Most come for Galleria Umberto's signature item, a deeply satisfying square slice of Sicilian pizza topped with a zingy sauce and a blanket of charred mozzarella. You can have any kind of pizza you want—as long as it is plain cheese—because that is the only kind Galleria Umberto makes. It's served room temperature from the ancient oven-worn tray it was cooked in—direct to your paper plate. And because Galleria Umberto is so popular, the pizza turns over quickly, which guarantees you'll always get a fresh slice.

North End resident Umberto Deuterio founded the restaurant in 1974; he named it after himself and the famous Galleria Umberto

shopping arcade in his native Naples. The old gents who run Galleria Umberto today are his sons: brothers Paul, Ralph, and Anthony. Paul is the quiet oldest brother who works the counter. Ralph is more gregarious and is quick to speak Italian with the regulars, and Anthony works in the kitchen.

Vintage Spots: North End
V. CIRACE: EST. 1906

A handsome space, this is one of the oldest wine shops in the country, run by the Cirace family for generations. Brother-and-sister owners Jeff and Lisa Cirace are both passionate and approachable. Known for its commitment to northern Italian vintages, Cirace does some of its own importing, giving it access to a select line of boutique grappas and liquors you just won't find anywhere else.

173 North St.; (617) 227-3193; vcirace.com

Says Paul, "We were five kids. My father did construction and played in a band for the feasts. He opened this place because he had an army to work for him, and in those days, you didn't need a lot of money to get started."

Galleria Umberto relies on volume, rock-bottom pricing, and a menu that is as limited today as it was back in the day. Beside the trays of pizza, Galleria Umberto's hot case is neatly stacked with fried potato *panzarotti* (croquettes), panini, and a few types of calzones. Their *arancini* deserve special mention (and have many local foodie fans)—the deep-fried risotto balls are filled with a meat ragu, peas, and mozzarella and are almost as big as a *bocce pallino jack.*

Clearly, with the exception of the food, the Umberto "experience" comes with a few quirks. The restaurant is open only Monday through Saturday for lunch beginning at 11 a.m. If you come at noon, be prepared for long, slow-moving lines, and not surprisingly, it is cash only. The kitchen makes a certain amount of food every day and when the food is gone, they pull down the metal grating and the employees call it a day. Latecomers, you've been warned.

GERARD'S ADAMS CORNER

772 ADAMS ST. • DORCHESTER, MA 02124

(617) 282-637 • GERARDSADAMSCORNER.COM

The Center of Dorchester's Irish Village

*P*art restaurant, part convenience store, Gerard's Adams Corner knows its crowd—frequently by name—which has made this spot a Dorchester institution for more than 40 years.

Situated at the end of what was once the Adams Street trolley line, the first convenience store located here dates from 1908 and was known as the Sunny Side Waiting Room.

Current owner Gerard Adomunes is OFD (originally from Dorchester). "My father's parents came from Lithuania; my mother's parents came from Ireland." He was just 20 years old when he bought the Adams Corner store. "I was at Northeastern, playing football in 1969. I was majoring in physical education. I just wasn't happy."

Gerard had worked part-time at the little convenience store throughout high school and when he heard it was for sale he knew he could make a go of it. But he had to cobble together the financing. "Of course, I couldn't get a loan. My father had to sign for me. The owner took back some paper, and my brother gave me some money," Gerard recalls.

Gerard cleaned up the shop and transformed it into the neighborhood variety store. Adams Corner store also has the distinction of being one of the original agents for the Massachusetts State Lottery. "The lottery gave us a big boost," says Gerard.

Gerard says the store was the catalyst for his other business endeavors. In 1977 he bought the Adams Street property. He simultaneously bought Joseph's Luncheonette, located next door. "We closed the restaurant and remodeled the store. I opened the restaurant in

September 1977. But it was the Blizzard of '78 that made Gerard's. People had cabin fever and we were open. That's when Gerard's took off." Over the decades, Gerard's has grown tremendously. In 1983 the entire building was renovated including an addition to the restaurant to increase from 38 to 88 the number of seats. In 1996 Gerard obtained a full liquor license. And he started with just six employees and now numbers nearly 35 staff.

Gerard's is a homey, humble space and offers what the neighborhood wants: comfort food that's been, as Gerard puts it, "spruced up." The sizeable menu features burgers, salads, and sandwiches at lunch, prime rib, meat loaf, gourmet pizzas, and the ever-popular fish and chips at dinner. Gerard's signature menu item is its fry-up or full Irish breakfast, available every day. It comes complete with fried eggs, Irish bacon, Irish sausage, black sausage (pork sausage thickened with hog blood) and white pudding (similar but without the blood), home fries, and Irish brown bread.

Gerard's is also one of the leading retailers of Irish food products in the state. For a taste of the Emerald Isle at home, Gerard's Adams Corner store has aisle after aisle of goods imported from Ireland. The refrigerator is full of boiling bacon, sausages, butter, and

cheese. There is an entire wall dedicated to bags of crisps or potato chips. Taytos is the universally loved Irish brand and Gerard's stocks the addictive cheese and onion and the quirky prawn cocktail flavors. On the shelves you'll find tins of tomatoey Batchelor's Irish farm peas, Erin brand soups (oxtail is a favorite), Barry's Irish tea, McCambridge brown bread, and all manner of McVittie's biscuits (cookies) and Cadbury chocolates.

The only entrance to Gerard's is through the convenience store; it's a source of entertainment, mystery, and frustration for newcomers. Says Gerard, "It's how we know if someone has never been here before."

While many customers come from the surrounding neighborhood and nearby South Shore towns like Weymouth, Braintree, and Scituate (where 40 percent of the population is Irish-American), Gerard's also has regulars from all over New England including Cape Cod and New Hampshire.

Gerard's is the kind of restaurant that attracts multigenerational crowds, especially on weekends. Gerard says, "In the old days, pennies would slip between the floorboards in the store. Grownups come here with their children and remember how they used to try to pick up the pennies when they were kids." On a sad note, many people have come at a time of bereavement for a meal because this is where their dad or mom used to always go. "When I'm out in the neighborhood, people will stop me and say, 'Are you Gerard? I love your place.' It makes me feel good."

GROLIER POETRY BOOK SHOP

6 PLYMPTON ST. • CAMBRIDGE, MA 02138

(617) 547-4648 • GROLIERPOETRYBOOKSHOP.COM

One of the Country's Greatest Poetry Treasures

The Grolier is a literary landmark, the oldest exclusively poetry bookstore in the country and a much loved gathering place for the Harvard community. The selection, meanwhile, is something you'll never find on Amazon—a collection of 15,000 carefully selected volumes stacked in floor-to-ceiling bookcases, all either containing poetry or relating to poetry. There are books by poets of underrepresented cultures, anthologies of ancient poems in translation, modernist classics, and chapbooks by poets yet to be discovered.

Perhaps there can be no finer endorsement of the Grolier than the words of Pulitzer Prize-winning poet Robert Creeley: "Poetry is our final human language and resource. The Grolier is where poetry still lives, still talks, still makes the only sense that ever matters."

Entering from a side street around the corner from Harvard Square, climb the well-worn granite steps into a literary haven. It's a tiny space—just 404 square feet—but there is much history here.

Originally opened as a general bookstore in 1927 by Harvard alum Gordon Cairnie, the Grolier transitioned to a poetry-only store as early as 1929. Over the years, T. S. Eliot, E. E. Cummings, Allen Ginsburg, John Ashbery, and Robert Pinsky have all been patrons. Anyone who visited the store during the Cairnie years remembers the Grolier as a bookshop/library and as a de facto club for aspiring poets. A big old couch in the front window invited patrons to stay and browse—which greatly impressed a young Nigerian poet and Harvard graduate student named Ifeanyi Menkiti, who gave a reading here in 1969.

Ifeanyi is a presence—a big man with a deep voice that still retains an African lilt. He is a long-time philosophy professor at Wellesley College and author of two books of poetry: *Before a Common Soil* and *Of Altair, the Bright Light*. He bought the Grolier from Louisa Solano in 2006. Louisa had worked in the store since she was a teenager; in 1972 she purchased the Grolier from the Cairnie estate. Louisa worked tirelessly (and nearly single-handedly) for nearly 50 years sharing with the public her passion for poetry.

Owning a bookstore, surrounded by books and writers all day, is an almost romantic notion. This is a spare operation—other than

Ifeanyi and his wife, Carol, the store is staffed by just one additional full-time employee. Harvard University is the landlord. "They could raise the rent and chase us out, but so many people that are associated with the Grolier went to Harvard, it would be a public relations disaster," Ifeanyi says. Yet, the economics of owning a bookstore, let alone one devoted only to poetry, are challenging. "This is really a labor of love," says Ifeanyi.

Ifeanyi likes to tell the story of a young high school girl who spent hours in the store reading. "You could see the delight in her eyes. At the end of three hours, she didn't buy anything, but the joy in her face was the best sale of the day." Ifeanyi becomes particularly enthusiastic about the store's poetry readings, which promote the discovery that writing and reading poetry brings forth. "We've had some wonderful events. The poets talk about their work and the writing process. Afterwards, I try to engage the audience in discussion. I jokingly call them the Menkiti Seminars."

To build upon the Grolier's connection with the community and to ensure the store's future, Ifeanyi has established a nonprofit foundation. The Grolier imprint publishes the winners of the annual Grolier Discovery Awards for new poetry. The program recently expanded to include an Established Poets Series, recently publishing *So Spoke Penelope* by Chicano poet Tino Villanueva.

According to Ifeanyi, "In terms of the store's educational and cultural mission to advance poetry, we are doing a lot—the readings, discussions, the award series. But I'm not very business savvy. People really love this store and want it to succeed. My hope is that the foundation will get the store to the next century. It is important that the story of the Grolier bookshop continues to be told."

HARVARD BOOK STORE

1256 MASSACHUSETTS AVE. • CAMBRIDGE, MA 02138

(617) 661-1515 • HARVARD.COM

A Bookstore's Next Chapter

*R*eports of the demise of bookstores are greatly exaggerated. Just look at Cambridge's Harvard Book Store. One of the most well-known and respected independent bookstores in the country, the store is part literary salon and part living room for the Harvard Square community. It hosts more than 300 reading events a year that draw such legendary authors as David McCullough and Stephen King as well as of-the-moment writers like B.J. Novak and Amy Chua.

The ownership of the Harvard Book Store has only recently changed hands. Jeff Mayersohn is not a career bookseller. A former high-tech executive, he had little experience with bookstores, apart

from a passion for them, when he and his wife, Linda Seamonson, bought the store from Frank Kramer in 2008. Frank's father, Mark, had founded the store, a literary landmark, in Harvard Square in 1932. When Frank was looking to transition out of ownership, Jeff was able to realize a lifelong dream to own a bookstore. "My favorite recreational activity has always been to go to a bookstore and buy and read books," he says. "I first became a customer of this store when I came to Harvard as a freshman in 1969. It has always been my favorite bookstore."

Today what sets the Harvard Book Store apart is Jeff's modern approach to the book business. He's keen on moving the store forward, especially in terms of technology, while remaining committed to what Harvard's devoted customers value—the store's focus on community and a highly educated staff with a tireless enthusiasm for the written word.

Although Harvard is the store's landlord, the Harvard Book Store is not affiliated with the university (the campus bookstore is the

Harvard Coop, which is run by Barnes & Noble). Housed in an elegant brick and stone building dating from the early 1900s, over time the store has expanded to take over three adjacent storefronts and occupies more than 5,500 square feet of sales space.

The thoughtfully balanced inventory is noteworthy for its large range of general interest titles—including fiction and non—along with strong academic content, which is precisely what you would expect to find from a bookstore in the shadow of Harvard Yard. Thanks to its large expanse of front windows, the store is light and bright and is extremely welcoming to all kinds of readers. The staff is also fond of writing individual book reviews on cards taped to shelves throughout the store. The store's lower level offers secondhand books and remainders (discounted overstocks) at bargain prices.

In terms of competing with online book retailers, the Harvard Book Store has embraced technology. Not only does the store have an attractive website, but customers can purchase books directly from the store online. The store's staff—mostly young and just out of college or grad school—are passionate readers and masters of social media too, making Harvard Book Store's presence on Facebook and Twitter lighthearted, fun, and engaging. And while Amazon toys with the idea of delivery drones, the Harvard Book Store has been offering local customers same-day service since 2009. Says Jeff: "We can get books into the hands of our customers in a few hours, certainly in the same day with our bike delivery service."

Jeff is also enthusiastic about the digitization of books. One of the first things he did when buying the store was to install a compact digital press that utilizes print-on-demand technology. The Harvard Book Store has access to nearly 5 million titles including books in the public domain and out-of-print books. The store's custom printing machine, a robot named Paige M. Gutenborg or "Paige," is located right in the store and takes just five to seven minutes to print, bind, and trim a book. The finished paperback book is virtually identical to the publisher's original and sells at cover price. "In any given month we are printing a thousand books, of which half are previously published books. We also support a lot of self-publishing—books for authors as well as dissertations and theses for academics," says Jeff.

He is clearly delighted with his second career choice: "It is so much fun to own a bookstore. What's so wonderful about this business is that you can be working, or pretending that you are working, by chatting about books. There are some fascinating people who are customers of our store. And in our case, we also get to talk to the authors. Many of the people that we host at the store are people whose work I've admired forever. Although I am in my 60s, I just bought the business and I feel that I am going to do this for a long time."

HELEN'S LEATHER SHOP

110 CHARLES ST. • BOSTON, MA 02114

(617) 742-2077 • HELENSLEATHER.COM

Cowboy Cachet in the Heart of the Hill

J t's hard to picture proper Bostonians wearing cowboy boots—which makes it all the more incongruous that Helen's Leather Shop has thrived on blue-blooded Charles Street for more than 40 years.

Helen Bourgeois was a Beacon Hill icon. When she and her husband, Ed, founded the store that bears her name, in 1970, leather

wasn't as mainstream as it is today. Leather was for bikers and hippies—back then leather bomber jackets, moccasins, and Frye boots were all the rage. In those days, too, Charles Street was not nearly as exclusive as it is today and had a decidedly more Greenwich Village or Haight-Ashbury vibe.

Helen passed away in 2012 at the age of 90, leaving the store to her daughter Lisa Weller, a talented leather craftsperson in her own right. Behind the scenes, granddaughters Ali Dutson and Caitlyn Weller are also involved in the operation of the store. But the front man of the shop is Gregory Bournazos, who has been with Helen's Leather Shop since 1982 and is now the shop's general manager. He's a shopkeeper in the truest sense of the word: "I'm a Jack-of-all-trades—selling, ordering inventory, cleaning the store, and washing the windows," he says.

Carved out of an elegant brick town house that was once the home of John Albion Andrew, the Massachusetts governor during the Civil War, Helen's is actually a tiny shop. At just about 500 square feet, the store is not much bigger than a large walk-in closet.

Vintage Spot: Beacon Hill

GARY DRUG: EST. 1934

One of the few remaining independent drugstores around, this second-generation family-owned shop is a Beacon Hill institution. Hermann Greenfield bought this tiny neighborhood pharmacy in 1972; his son Dan Greenfield now owns the place. The wide-ranging inventory (from luxe Mason Pearson hairbrushes to hard-to-find medical equipment to prescriptions to all sorts of lotions and potions) makes it good; a pharmacy staff that takes the time to listen to and answer questions makes it great.

59 Charles St.; (617) 227-0023; garydrug.com

When you step inside the store, the whole place smells of leather, and soft jazz plays in the background. The store stocks basic leather items like kidskin gloves and fringed saddlebag purses. There are also cowboy shirts for adults and children that are popular with foreign visitors. The store's specialty is cowboy boots; its inventory ranges from $200 and can go as high as $2,000 and includes classic Lucchese and Justin brand boots as well as high-end contemporary showstoppers made from alligator and ostrich by Liberty. And as you would expect from authentic western wear, almost all the goods are made in America.

There's also a far smaller but still fine collection of cowboy hats (Stetsons are very popular), leather jackets, belts, and belt buckles—many of which are made of silver and turquoise.

Over the years, the store has evolved to include more western wear. Gregory describes how in the 1970s a couple of cowboy boots were added to the inventory and over time, more cowboy things have slowly been added to the mix. "Organically we grew out of a niche in the market that we found and enjoyed selling; now the store is nearly 75 percent cowboy and 25 percent leather." Gregory describes the clientele as largely international. "They want to take home something with them that reminds them of the United States. A big part of that is the cowboy culture that they associate with America."

The store is also known to attract celebrities coming through town—Stevie Wonder, Twiggy, and Wayne Newton have all bought from the store. King Abdullah of Jordan was a customer when he was a student in the area. Several of the members of Boston's home-grown rock bands, Aerosmith and the J. Geils Band, are customers. And years ago, when Keith Lockhart needed a cowboy hat at the last minute for a Fourth of July Esplanade Pops concert, Helen's Leather Shop delivered.

Gregory spends time with his customers, offering a helping hand when selecting styles and determining fit (which makes all the difference), as well as giving advice on leather care. He explains, "We don't do anything on the Internet. Leather jackets and cowboy boots are not everyday purchases. Our customers typically need some guidance." Shop at Helen's, and you can be sure that you will walk away with exactly the right cowboy boots for you.

IRVING'S TOY & CARD SHOP

371 HARVARD AVE. • BROOKLINE, MA 02446

(617) 566-9327

A Quintessential Neighborhood Toy Store

A white and candy-apple-red striped awning heralds the entrance, and a bell gently jingles each time the door opens and closes at this charming toy shop.

Tucked between two apartment buildings in Brookline's Coolidge Corner, Irving's Toy & Card Shop has served generation after generation of neighborhood children. The shop's owner, Ethel Weiss, always

sits just inside the entrance, wearing a smock with a button that says, "I love my customers." And she clearly does. At 99 years old, she leaves her apartment next door every morning to work in the small shoebox size store, just as she has every day for the past 75 years.

Ethel and her husband, Irving Kravetz, bought what was once a grocery storefront in 1939; by 1948 they were able to buy the building. "It gradually evolved into a toy and candy store because of the school nearby," says Ethel, referring to the Edward Devotion School. Affectionately called "Devo" in the neighborhood, the school has as its most famous student John F. Kennedy, who attended kindergarten through third grade there.

Irving passed away in 1960, leaving Ethel with two young daughters. Ethel married Abe Weiss in 1962 and they ran the store together until Abe's passing in 1981. "Since that time, I've kept on with it . . . " Ethel says, trailing off.

When school lets out at 2:30, a rush of kids swarm the store to spend their allowance money. Most head straight to the candy counter in the front of the store that is full of classic treats: Mallo Cups,

Now & Laters, Hershey bars, and Jujubes. Ethel has each child add up their purchase in their head: "The kids learn their arithmetic here. I always have them count out their change with me."

As for toys, you won't find any new-fangled electronic doodads here. What you will find: pinwheels, jump ropes, kaleidoscopes, coloring books, board games, and bags of marbles that appeal to kids and parents alike. Among the store's most popular items are Ethel's self-published posters, "Thoughts for a Happier Life" and "How to Be Old and Still Be Happy," which she personalizes and autographs for each buyer in her still steady hand. Some of her tips: Show appreciation. Try to be a good role model. Eat sensibly and obey good health rules. Enjoy being yourself. Ethel often has her young customers read the posters out loud. "I try to encourage the right things for my customers. They are wonderful kids and their parents care," she says.

The store is a sentimental favorite for longtime residents who are old enough to remember when candy at Irving's was just a penny; they stop in when they are in the area to talk to Ethel and reminisce. According to Ethel, kids haven't changed much over the generations. "They buy just about the same toys today as they always have."

Asked about the store's success, Ethel says, "I don't overcharge for one thing and I try to think of the needs of my customers." As for retirement, Ethel won't hear of it. "I hope that I am able to work awhile longer. I'm going to be 100 in August."

JACOB WIRTH

31–39 STUART ST. • BOSTON, MA 02116
(617) 338-8586 • JACOBWIRTH.COM

To German Fare: *Prost!*

Founded in 1868 during the heyday of beer halls in America, Jacob Wirth is the only remaining German restaurant in Boston, and the third oldest restaurant in the city. Generation after generation of Bostonians has enjoyed Jacob Wirth's spirited *gemütlichkeit* style of dining: good food, good drink, and good company. Located in Boston's Theater District, "Jake's" attracts Suffolk and Emerson students and workers from Tufts New England Medical Center, as well as tourists who come for German comfort food and piano sing-alongs fueled by free-flowing beer.

Current owner Kevin Fitzgerald enjoys telling visitors the story behind Jacob Wirth's ambience: "You walk in through double doors. In front of you is a 90-foot-long bar, round mahogany tables, bentwood chairs, a piano player, wainscoting, and a high ceiling. It is every saloon in every western movie that you ever watched. There used to be a very large German population in Texas, so all the westerns are based on German beer halls like Jake's."

Jacob Wirth was born to a family of winegrowers from the town of Kreuzach in Germany's Rhineland. When he immigrated to the US and arrived in Boston, Jacob established the original Jacob Wirth restaurant across the street from its current Stuart Street location. Today two distinct bow-front town houses make up the restaurant; Jacob bought the first one in 1871 and the next-door building in 1890. In those days, Jacob Wirth thrived serving hearty dishes like pig's knuckles, beef tongue, and plates of pickled herring along with giant steins of beer.

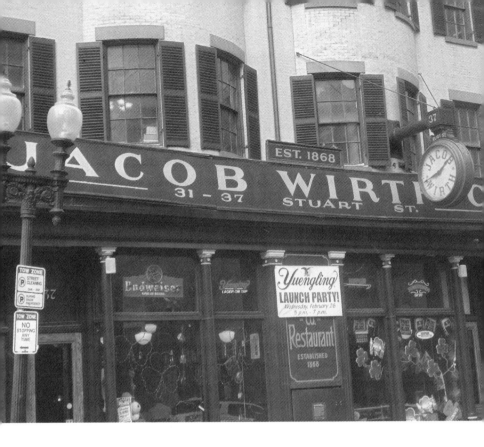

It is said that at one time or another Jacob and his brother Henry had financial interests in as many as three breweries and 20 restaurants throughout New England including Providence, Worcester, and Springfield, along with Boston. Notably, Jacob Wirth was from the same town as Ebehard Anheuser, co-founder of the beer company that eventually became Anheuser-Busch, and he secured one of the first licenses to distribute Anheuser-Busch products.

When Jacob Wirth passed away in 1892, his widow ran the business until her own death in 1899. Their son, also named Jacob Wirth, dropped out of Harvard to take over the restaurant in 1902. Jacob Wirth's struggled in the early 20th century with the outbreak of World War I, widespread anti-German sentiment, and the onset of Prohibition. For 13 long years, Jacob Wirth's served "near beer" and operated largely as Boston's legal speakeasy. "Everyone thinks that beer wasn't legal during Prohibition. But actually, 3.2 percent beer was allowed. Jacob Wirth's never closed its doors and always operated within the limits of the law," Kevin proudly explains.

The junior Jacob Wirth ran the restaurant until his death in 1963 and was succeeded by his son-in-law Frank Lindsay until 1975, when ownership of the restaurant passed to the Fitzgerald family.

William Fitzgerald, Kevin's father, bought the business, literally, in a fire sale. In the old days, part of the charm of Jacob Wirth's was the sawdust on the floor. In those days too, patrons smoked in restaurants. One evening a stray cigarette smoldered overnight and in the morning, the floor of the dining room was gone; the tables and chairs were sitting on the joists. The restaurant was closed for three weeks for repairs. "My father had many businesses, and one of them was contracting. When Jacob Wirth's reopened, no one came and Mrs. Wirth declared bankruptcy. My father realized that he would be getting just 30 cents on the dollar for his work, so instead he bought the business."

The Fitzgerald family has remained true to Jacob Wirth's heritage while improving the place. "When we bought the restaurant there was only one beer vendor, and you had the choice between light lager or dark lager," says Kevin. The third generation of Fitzgeralds is already making an impact at the restaurant. Meaghan Fitzgerald, Kevin's daughter, is Jacob Wirth's general manager and has recently been named one of *Food Service Report*'s "40 Under 40 Rising Stars."

As you would expect in a beer hall, wurst is indeed the thing to order: bratwurst (beef and pork), knockwurst (pork), and weisswurst (veal) are all outstanding and served with a traditional German potato salad. More ambitious dinner fare includes wiener schnitzel, which is served with dill spaetzel and a lemon butter sauce and an authentic sauerbraten served with ginger snap gravy and red cabbage. Today there are a lot more than two beers at Jacob Wirth's. A wide selection of nearly 50 American and German beers on tap and another 40 to 50 different bottles gives customers a choice among 100 different beers, ensuring an Oktoberfest atmosphere every night and that Jacob Wirth's continues to be a Theater District tradition.

J.J. FOLEY'S

117 E. BERKLEY ST. • BOSTON, MA 02118
(617) 728-9101 • JJFOLEYSCAFE.COM

A Storied Boston Pub for Lifting a Pint

J.J. Foley's has been around since 1909 and it really takes no imagination at all to picture the place as it was more than 100 years ago. From the long, mirror-backed mahogany bar showcasing fine whiskeys (there are no stools here, since "real men" should stand as they drink), to the gilded tin ceiling, exposed brick, and a decor that features a dartboard and both the American flag and the Irish tricolor, J.J. Foley's is an almost perfect period piece.

With the removal of the elevated Orange Line T in the 1980s and the end of rent control in the early 1990s, this portion of Boston's South End has transformed over the years from a seedy, working-class enclave into one of the trendiest sections of the city. Through it all, J.J. Foley's has always been a neighborhood bar, uniting folks of all ages and backgrounds in a laid-back atmosphere; a place where personal troubles are shed—if only for a couple of hours. Doctors and nurses from nearby Boston Medical Center, city workers, union guys,

newspaper reporters, and hard-drinking politicians all come for a few rounds—and it makes for great people-watching. This all just goes to prove that a business does not have to be young to be hip.

Jerry Foley is the third-generation owner of J.J. Foley's, which was founded by his grandfather Jeremiah J. Foley, who immigrated to Boston from County Kerry. "My grandfather never missed work; he never closed. We even stayed open during 13 years of Prohibition, which was quite a feat," Jerry says.

Dressed in a crisp white dress shirt, tie, and apron, Jerry is a genial but hard-nosed publican who runs a welcoming bar and is able to banter with the regulars while keeping a wary eye out for who is coming in the front door. Jerry has devoted much of his life to serving his loyal customers; he's at the bar six nights a week and on any given day he is joined behind the bar by one or more of his sons. "I'm just the caretaker," he likes to say.

But Jerry is quick to let you know that he is the father of seven; four of the Foley boys—Michael, Patrick, Jeremiah, and Brendan— work either full- or part-time at J.J. Foley's; another son is a priest

in Baltimore. Daughter Meagan is a nurse, while his other daughter, Caitlin, works for the state in the probation office.

Devoted to J.J. Foley's continued existence, Jerry's kids have embraced change to help redefine the pub for the future. There are well-pulled pints—Guinness, Smithwick's, and Harp, of course, along with a dozen or so local and international drafts that run from the taps. And no longer does the bar just serve toasted sandwiches for the regulars. In 2007 the family bought the space next door and added a cozy restaurant that serves more-than-respectable pub fare, like homemade beef and lamb shepherd's pie and grilled Scottish salmon with sautéed seasonal vegetables. Conversational chat still rules at J.J. Foley's, but now a couple of flat-screens are discreetly mounted on the walls, so you'll never miss a Red Sox game.

Over the years, J.J. Foley's has also become something of a political landmark. A plaque on the building honors the Boston police strike of 1919, which was voted on by members in the Union Hall above J.J. Foley's—and quelled by then Massachusetts governor Calvin Coolidge, gaining him national attention for a future presidential run. Harkening back to the machine politics that ruled Boston in the early 20th century, the walls are lined with political memorabilia from decades of city history, including framed campaign posters from legendary Boston pols James Michael Curley, Kevin White, and Ray Flynn. There is sports memorabilia too, including an autographed picture of Ted Williams. Back in the day, John L. Sullivan, the first heavyweight champion of the world, was a frequent customer. Pointing to Sullivan's photograph, Jerry says, "He was Boston strong."

The neighborhood has changed a lot since the first Jeremiah Foley poured a glass of whiskey more than a century ago. And in that time, J.J. Foley's has changed little. "This is the oldest family-run bar in the United States of America," says Jerry. "When you put your name outside, that means something. You have a reputation to uphold."

KEEZER'S CLASSIC CLOTHING

140 RIVER ST. • CAMBRIDGE, MA 02139
(617) 547-2455 • KEEZERS.COM

Men's Formal Wear on a Budget

What do Franklin D. Roosevelt, Allen Ginsberg, and the Winklevoss twins have in common? They have all shopped at Keezer's, a classic menswear store offering good quality new and used tailored clothing and accessories at reasonable prices.

What Keezer's lacks in atmosphere—industrial clothing racks and harsh fluorescent lighting—it makes up for with its vast selection. The store, a fixture of the Harvard/Cambridge community for more than a century, is famous for its formal wear, from tuxedos available for rent or purchase including entry-level Calvin Klein and Ralph Lauren to flashy high-end brands like Zanieri. "Virtually every year when the Nobel prizes are awarded we get men in to buy or rent white tie and tails for the ceremonies in Sweden," says current owner Len Goldstein. And if a guy doesn't realize his event is black-tie, in a pinch Keezer's can get him tuxed in a few hours.

Len Goldstein has owned Keezer's for more than three decades. Born in nearby Chelsea and raised in Winthrop, Len first worked in retail as a teenager in the family liquor store. "It was illegal for me to work, of course, but my father would give me a list of inventory to bring out. He taught me how to rotate stock and how to make change."

Founded in 1895 by brothers Max and Joe Keezer, the original Keezer's was located in Harvard Square. According to Len, back in those days, 17 men's handmade clothing stores in the Square catered to Harvard students. "A lot of the students grew up in families that made their money in mining, ranching, and railroads. Their fathers

would send them east for a gentleman's education and they would give them a clothing allowance, but they wouldn't give them a lot of money for debauchery. The kids would have some suits of clothing made, and then sell their nearly new clothing to Keezer's and get money for booze, for clubs, and for dates."

"By 1960, Joe Keezer couldn't schlep the merchandise anymore so he took on Fred Salo as a partner," says Len, who bought the company from Fred in 1978. "I promised him that I would keep the business as close to the original way as I could. When I bought the business, the stock was depleted, so we bought a famous name and a two-year lease."

Len moved Keezer's to its present-day Central Square location in 1986. "Between Harvard and MIT, we've had a lot of famous people shop here." Today Keezer's is the biggest name in the Boston men's discount clothing business. The stock is a mix of new and old, and everything is priced at wholesale or below. Remember Seinfeld's puffy shirt? You can buy one here, still in its package. There are natty fedoras, Mad Men–era skinny ties, and to-be-tied bow ties. Department

store surplus is another Keezer specialty. "I buy new things when I can get them at clearance," says Len. Among the finds is a large selection of name-brand dress shirts, designer suits in superfine wool, dress-for-success sports coats, and Italian silk ties. "We get a lot of students and we get a lot of extremely wealthy people who want a good value. We also get a lot of funky people. It's the nature of used stuff; it tends to draw people that are different."

When it comes to their clothes, most men can use a little help. Thankfully, the knowledgeable salesmen at Keezer's are experts at schooling their customers on cut and fit. Even if a man doesn't know his way around a dressing room, he will walk out of Keezer's looking as though he does—and with a couple of bills still in his pockets.

KENMORE ARMY NAVY

477 WASHINGTON ST. • BOSTON, MA 02111

(617) 292-2769

Boston's Headquarters for Military Goods and Other Cool Stuff

*A*n '80s classic rock sound track featuring J. Geils and Santana plays in the background of this musty, chaotic store that specializes in authentic military gear, work wear, and gadgets. This is one of only a few Boston-area military surplus stores still around.

Kenmore Army Navy is a small space, but packed to the rafters with all sorts of useful things, from discounted Converse All-Stars to gas masks to navy-style pea coats to duffel bags, Swiss Army knives, and everything camo—and all at super-low prices. Troll through the store long enough and you will find some things you never knew you needed—parachute cord and used military footlockers—but whose use (car trunk emergency rope? coffee table base?) will suggest itself to you eventually.

The entertainment value of Kenmore Army Navy is considerable. The clientele for military gear tends to be the young and tattooed: students, hipsters, and even local drifters. Downtown workers come in for scrubs (in nearly every color), chef's clothing, and durable Dickies work pants. There are also good deals on camping gear like tents and army cots. At Halloween, this is a great place to pick up hats and other accessories for one-of-a-kind costumes like Indiana Jones, Che Guevara, or anyone from the *Duck Dynasty* crew. The store also does a good business supplying props and costumes for Boston's Theater District and the Hollywood movie industry when there is filming in

KENMORE ARMY & NAVY STORE

477

Timberland
PRO
PRO SERIES

carhartt

- **Workwear**
  - **Raingear**
  - **Camping**
    Supplies

Dickies

Dickies

Girl

Levi's

- Me
- Wo
- Chil

town. Among the celebrities who have shopped here are Steven Tyler, Shaquille O'Neal, Mark Wahlberg, and Cicely Tyson.

Owner Jerry Blocher started Kenmore Army Navy from scratch in 1976. "I went to Boston University for a while, but I never really knew what I wanted to do. I worked part-time for Snyder's Army Navy for seven or eight years and I liked it, so I opened my own store in Kenmore Square. I was there for 22 years."

Jerry scours the market for new, used, and surplus items for the store. Over the years, the Army Navy business has changed from selling military surplus from the Vietnam War to supplying practical work clothing to becoming a favorite depot for urban fashion trendsetters. "We sell a little of everything but after nearly 40 years in the business, I've learned what sells," he says.

The store has been in its current location, at the edge of Boston's Chinatown, for nearly nine years, just down the street from the now-defunct Snyder's, where Jerry got his start. He says, "Business is fantastic. Look at all the people outside. When you've got that many people walking by your store, if you're not doing good business, something is wrong."

KUPEL'S BAKERY

421 HARVARD ST. • BROOKLINE, MA 02446

(617) 566-9528 • KUPELSBAKERY.COM

The Best Boston Bagel Is Out of Town

𝔍 t's really not that surprising that the best bagels in Boston require a trek to neighboring Brookline—the city many consider to be the hub of the Jewish community in New England. Along Brookline's quaint main street, this small corner shop with the hand-bent neon sign is a welcome beacon that draws longtime customers and tourists (usually visiting the nearby John F. Kennedy Birthplace National Historic Site) for quite possibly some of the best bagels outside of New York.

Kupel's, pronounced "couples," is a play on the name of the store's founders. The bakery was established in 1978 by local resident Allan Kupelnick and his wife, Diane. "Since it was owned by Allan and Diane, they decided to call it Kupel's," explains current owner Farzad Ghorbi.

Farzad is a bagel man via Iran, yet these are utterly authentic Jewish bagels. Farzad grew up Muslim in a largely Jewish and Armenian neighborhood in Tehran. He cut his teeth in the business as a new immigrant; beginning in 1983 he worked with the Kupelnicks as their bakery manager and in 2007 was offered the opportunity to buy the business from them.

Kupel's bagels are hand-rolled, kettle boiled, and baked on the premises. These beauties are something near bagel perfection: not too large, they are both crunchy and just chewy enough. Made throughout the day (the bakers come in at 2 a.m.), they are almost always available warm out of the oven.

Farzad is extremely proud of Kupel's product line. The bagel selection rivals that of any New York bagelry, with 22 flavors including

cinnamon glaze, whole wheat onion, and their best-selling every-thing bagel. There's an equally impressive choice of 30 cream cheese spreads, too, like honey walnut, the very popular Miami lox (with scallions), and even tofu cream cheese for vegans. Kupel's is known as well for its bagel specialty sandwiches like the Tom Brady—a winning combination of Atlantic smoked salmon, tomato, and chive cream cheese on a sesame seed bagel. In giant over-packed glass bakery cases, the shop offers a full spread of classic Jewish pastries from lemony pound cake, to dense chocolate rugelach, to fluffy brioche-like challah.

Kupel's is a no-frills kind of place, you might have to squeeze by others in line to see the bagel bins and order, and there's barely anywhere to sit, but with bagels and baked goods this good, no frills are necessary.

"When I started, we were an extremely busy store. Some nights we were open until 2 a.m. We were not just the 'Best of Boston' year

after year, but back then we were more or less the only true Boston bagel bakery," recalls Farzad. But through the years, Kupel's business has changed. "The blue-collar customer left when rent control left. And people are eating differently; they're not eating as much bread," he says.

Farzad is the father of three grown sons; the two younger boys have worked at the bakery behind the scenes occasionally during college, helping with the advertising, answering e-mail, and setting up the store's Facebook and Twitter accounts. Asked about the chance of a second generation taking over Kupel's, Farzad leaves the door open. "One day, down the road, if they feel that they want it, it's theirs."

The bakery is closed for Shabbat, so don't plan to go on a Saturday. Farzad has chosen to keep Kupel's kosher: "It's important for our customers." "We also use all the original recipes with no preservatives or additives. I wouldn't touch a good thing," he says. Kupel's certainly stands up to the neighborhood's high standards—the Sunday morning line of faithful customers out the door pretty much says it all.

LEAVITT & PEIRCE

1316 MASSACHUSETTS AVE. • CAMBRIDGE, MA 02138

(617) 547-0576 • LEAVITT-PEIRCE.COM

A Proud Throwback to a More Tolerant Time

This well-stocked tobacconist is less smoke shop than historic landmark. Entering Leavitt & Peirce, a fixture in Harvard Square since 1883, is like being transported back to another era.

Pass beneath the antique wooden Indian maiden statue over the front door and enter a large, crowded space where manly smells—the rich scents of tobacco, leather, and musk—permeate. From the metal

ceiling to the wood paneling and time-worn floors, this place lives and breathes old-school tobacconist shop.

Founded by Fred Leavitt and Waldo Peirce (their portraits hang prominently in the store), in its early years Leavitt & Peirce was considered a "den of iniquity" for generations of pipe-smoking and billiards-playing Harvard upperclassmen.

The shop's clutter of Harvard memorabilia—vintage footballs, autographed baseball team photos, and antique crew oars—is a reminder of those halcyon days. Today the lofted lounge is off-limits for smoking, but you can play a quiet game of chess here.

Leavitt & Peirce has always been a family-owned shop, having changed hands only four times in its entire history. The family of the current proprietor, Paul MacDonald, has owned Leavitt & Peirce since the late 1970s. Affable and chatty, Paul has worked in the business since he was a teenager. He is a second-generation tobacconist, following in his father's footsteps.

College students have always been, and still are, occasional cigar smokers. "When the weather is warm, our cigar sales are phenomenal," says Paul. Most of his customers are young people from area universities, including Harvard, Boston University, and Tufts University. Professors and workers associated with Harvard come in, as do tourists and smoking aficionados from all around the world. Paul says, "More people smoke than you would think."

As for famous customers, Paul won't say other than to mention that Nobel Prize winners and American presidents have all crossed Leavitt & Peirce's threshold. "Our kind of fame is different than most, but we treat everyone the same."

The staff are knowledgeable tobacconists all, and will gladly describe the properties of this cigar or that, give you tips on rolling your own cigarettes, or set you up with a hand-carved pipe and the supplies and instructions for smoking it. "We take our time with new pipe smokers," says Paul.

Even nonsmokers can appreciate much of what this shop has to offer. Spend some time poking about and you'll find that the original 100-year-old display cases are filled with an astonishing array of merchandise you cannot find just anywhere. Besides tobacco and tobacco accessories, the store offers classic men's gifts like cuff links, wallets, pens, and pewter flasks. There is a section of traditional

games as well, including chess, backgammon, playing cards, and poker chips. "If a game hasn't been around for at least 100 years, then we probably don't carry it," says Paul. Recently there has been a resurgence of interest in the art of shaving. According to Paul, all you need is a safety razor, soap, and a shave brush. "Some things can't be improved."

And whether a smoker or not, everyone is drawn to the tobacco bar. A tiered wooden counter groans under the weight of a dozen or so large glass jars containing hand-blended pipe tobacco with names like "Cake Box" and "Judge's Mixture"—just lift the lids and inhale.

Paul laments the gentrification of Harvard Square. "Today, students want banks, cell phone stores, and fast food restaurants. Harvard Square may have lost some of its character, but we don't want the Square to lose its characters." Certainly, Leavitt & Peirce and Paul MacDonald represent the best of quirky, colorful Harvard Square.

MAMMA MARIA

3 NORTH SQUARE • BOSTON, MA 02113
(617) 523-0077 • MAMMAMARIA.COM

Skillful, Passionate Stewardship
Through the Years

*D*on't let the clichéd name fool you: Mamma Maria is a Boston culinary landmark and one of the city's most celebrated restaurants for its intriguing Italian menu, unflinching service, and impeccable wine list.

This North End neighbor to Paul Revere's house is indeed a special place. Set in an elegant (but not overly formal) 1820s-era town house with candlelit tables dressed in crisp linens and a subtle decor in soft cream, celadon, and gold, this is easily one of the most romantic spots in the city.

As early as 1870, the once-grand little house was already cut up and turned into several storefronts including at one time a funeral home and an apartment building, explains John McGee, Mamma Maria's current owner. His is not an uncommon story: A freshly minted college graduate takes the leap and changes his career to follow a passion and with hard work and a lot of luck creates a runaway hit.

John's restaurant career began in 1984. After graduating from Middlebury College and contemplating medical school, he showed up at the door of Mamma Maria to work as a waiter, just as it was reopening under new management, "because living in your parents' basement wasn't as fashionable then as it is now," jokes John, now a father himself of two college-age daughters.

At that time Mamma Maria was transitioning from a noisy, red-sauce Italian-American joint to a more upscale Italian restaurant. It may seem like standard fare now, but handmade pasta and seasonal

authentic Italian food was rare in the 1980s. It helped, too, that just eight months after reopening, Mamma Maria was reviewed by *Gourmet* magazine. "At the time *Gourmet* just did New York City and San Francisco. They wrote a little piece on Boston and reviewed L'Espalier (pre–Frank McClelland), Seasons at the Bostonian Hotel helmed by a then-unknown chef named Lydia Shire, and us. Nine months into this interesting interlude and all of a sudden we had titans of industry and nationally known personalities at Mamma Maria. That was what sucked me in—that was the kick start."

John waited tables at Mamma Maria for a year, eventually managing the restaurant. In 1988 he was offered the opportunity to buy it. Like the dining room itself, the menu offers a balance of sophistication and comfort, haute technique, and everyday Italian cooking. The ingredients are impeccable and mostly from New England. John says, "Local is very fashionable right now, but the Italians almost invented it. We shop the season and the market. We don't buy anything from far away. We serve only Atlantic fish. I don't care what they serve in Italy; I'm not going to bring that. That would not be in the spirit of Italian food."

The menu changes often; in some cases you might find minor menu alterations daily. But regulars know that the pappardelle pasta with braised rabbit and the osso buco with saffron risotto are nearly always on the menu. In the winter the menu skews northern Italian, while in late July and August, the dishes represent more southern Italian cuisine. "Italians come here and completely get this restaurant," says John.

Over the years, the restaurant has carved out quite a following among locals as the go-to for special occasions. "We get the entire family cycle: a 16-year-old daughter's birthday party, a wedding rehearsal dinner, a 50th birthday party for Mom, an 80th birthday for Grandpa." Mamma Maria is also a magnet for the city's power brokers. John is loath to name names but points out the smallest of the restaurant's private dining rooms and mentions that the Patriots are still in Foxboro (and not in Hartford) "because of a meeting that happened there." All of Massachusetts is grateful.

Even after 30 years, Mamma Maria remains one of the most exciting dining destinations in Boston. About the future, John becomes thoughtful: "My wife and I seized on the idea early on, having traveled a lot, that especially in Europe there is this idea of a restaurant that goes on for a really long time and if anything it continues to get better. I hope I can do this forever."

MR. BARTLEY'S

1246 MASSACHUSETTS AVE. • CAMBRIDGE, MA 02138

(617) 354-6559 • MRBARTLEY.COM

Boston's Best Burgers Are in Cambridge

For many, Mr. Bartley's is the granddaddy of Boston-area burger joints, an unprepossessing Cambridge original that is renowned for its eclectic dorm-style decor—wood-paneled walls plastered with posters, political bumper stickers, purloined road signs, and various knickknacks. Located directly across from Harvard's Holyoke Gate, Mr. Bartley's attracts all that is Harvard Square—a mix of earnest students, tweedy professors, tourists, and blue-collar locals.

Vintage Spots: Cambridge
SCHOENHOF'S: EST. 1856

Another favorite of the ex-pat and academic communities, Schoenhof's has brought the world to Harvard Square and is the oldest and largest foreign bookstore in the country. Since 1983, the store has occupied the basement space of a historical 1930s brick town house. Besides fiction and nonfiction books in 50 languages, there's a delightful selection of foreign children's books including translations of Dr. Seuss and Harry Potter as well as easy reading novels for the high school Latin student. The vast reference section comprises dictionaries and all the latest learning materials for an array of languages from Spanish to Eskimo to Korean.

76A Mount Auburn St.; (617) 547-8855; schoenhofs.com

Mr. Bartley's biggest claim to fame is its hamburgers; plump seven-ounce patties of 100 percent chuck offered in as many as 60 variations, each reasonably priced and served with a side of sarcasm: the People's Republic of Cambridge ("liberal heaven") is topped with coleslaw and Russian dressing, while the iPhone ("Siri-ously delicious, ask her") comes with boursin cheese and grilled mushrooms and onions.

Some of the burgers are named for sports figures (the Big Papi, the Tom Brady); many are named for Harvard heavyweights or national political figures—which are often one and the same (the Barack Obama, the Mitt Romney, the Henry Louis "Skip" Gates Jr.). Asked what will get you on the menu, second-generation owner Bill Bartley says, "Do something stupid, do something smart, or just fly in the face of the liberal Cambridge wackos." When Bartley's has named a sandwich for you, surely it's a sign that you've made it.

Bill's parents, Joe and Joan Bartley, bought the old Harvard Spa when it was a convenience store and lunch counter, converting the space to Mr. Bartley's Burger Cottage in 1960, the year Bill was born.

Vintage Spots: Cambridge

THE COOP: EST. 1882

Originally set up as a student cooperative, the Coop (it's pronounced as one syllable) is Harvard's official bookstore. The main building dates from 1925 and still has lots of character—the columned entrance leads to a four-story library-like space with a grand spiral staircase and floor-to-ceiling bookcases stocked with best sellers and literary classics. The next-door annex sells Harvard apparel galore.

1400 Massachusetts Ave.; (617) 499-2000; thecoop.com

LA FLAMME: EST. 1898

Located in Harvard Square and said to be the oldest barbershop in Massachusetts, this classic eight-chair shop was opened by a French Canadian immigrant by the name of Arthur La Flamme. Since 1978, the shop has been owned by George Papalimberis, who counts among his clients some of Harvard's biggest names, among them Barack Obama while he attended Harvard Law.

21 Dunster St.; (617) 354-8377

OUT OF TOWN NEWS: EST. 1928

Located in the center of the Harvard Square traffic island, this iconic kiosk was once the MBTA station entrance and has operated as a newsstand here since 1955. If you like the smell of fresh newsprint or the crackle of magazine glossies, this is a browser's dream with an astonishing selection of domestic and international publications and journals. If you simply must have the *India Times, Elle France,* or *New African* magazine, it's here.

Zero Harvard Square; (617) 354-1441

It has always been a family business; growing up, Bill, his sister, and three brothers all worked in the restaurant at one time or another. Family still keeps Bartley's going; Joe and Joan come in for a couple of hours nearly every day; Bill's wife works in the restaurant two days a week as well.

Bill has been wielding a spatula at Bartley's since he was 14 years old. He is Bartley's head chef—a true grill master who on a good Saturday can sling 800 patties cooked to order from the well-seasoned flat-top grill. Bartley's other specialties include frappes (what New Englanders call milk shakes) that are so thick you need a spoon, and refreshing lime rickeys made from soda water, simple syrup, and fresh lime juice. Their onion rings are perfect—a tangle of fried cornmeal-crusted goodness. Bartley's sweet potato fries are tremendously popular too. "We've been doing sweet potato fries for 30 years now, way ahead of everybody else," says Bill.

Harvard Square hasn't changed and it has changed a lot, according to Bill. "Students used to eat three meals a day here. We are still always busy, but these days we are a destination restaurant; sometimes people come here right from the airport."

Now Boston is not immune to the recent nationwide proliferation of new burger joints—both fancy and plain. And there are nearly 10 other spots in Harvard Square alone that serve hamburgers. So what about the competition? "It's never been a problem," says Bill with a laugh. "They come and they go."

Six days a week (Bartley's is closed on Sunday), a steady stream of customers attests to Bartley's fan base of hungry college students and tourists. The line builds quickly, so especially on weekends, be prepared to wait for up to an hour for the privilege of a Bartley's hamburger. You'll sit elbow-to-elbow in a noisy and chaotic dining room. And Bartley's is also cash only—which only adds to the restaurant's charm.

"The secret to our success is luck as much as anything," Bill says. "But like my father says, you need dedication and perseverance too." And after more than five decades, Bartley's straightforward hamburgers are classic—just like the place that makes them.

Hitting All the Right Notes

*M*usic enthusiasts and professional musicians come from all around the country and all over the world to buy their pianos in Boston. Located at the corner of Tremont and Boylston Streets, between the Boston Common and the Theater District, the six-story limestone and brick Beaux Arts beauty is the home of M. Steinert & Sons, the oldest continuously operating music store in America.

Built in 1896 and named Steinert Hall, this became the headquarters for the then burgeoning music company. Steinert Hall quickly became a center of cultural life in Boston—and it was good for piano sales. Located on Piano Row, at a time when every major American city had a designated district of showrooms that represented the major piano manufacturers of the day, "We became the anchor store of Piano Row. Even when I came here in 1969, there were five other piano stores on this block. Now we are the only one left," says Paul Murphy, who runs the business along with his brother Jerome.

M. Morris Steinert, a German immigrant who arrived in America in 1850, founded Steinert & Sons. Initially, he made his living making and selling eyeglasses door-to-door. But his avocation was music, having learned to play the piano and organ in a monastery in his native Bavaria. Then, as now, it wasn't easy to make a living as a musician. Morris gave music lessons, repaired instruments, and worked as a performer. He opened the doors to his first piano shop (selling used instruments) in Athens, Georgia, in 1860. The Civil War forced a move to the Northeast and the opening of a piano store in New Haven,

Connecticut, in 1865. By 1869 he had received a coveted "agency" to represent piano manufacturer Steinway, whose pianos were considered then, as now, among the finest in the world.

M. Steinert & Sons is in fact the world's second oldest dealer for Steinway and enjoyed almost immediate success because of its association with the brand. Pianos came of age in the Victorian era. When Steinway pianos were introduced in the 1850s, the company's acoustic and mechanical improvements (Steinway holds more than 120 patents) practically created the piano industry. Today Steinway pianos still have an ardent following among musicians, both amateur and professional, for their sound and beauty.

In the late 19th and early 20th centuries, pianos were the center of entertainment in every middle-class American home. By 1883, Morris had opened piano stores throughout New England, including his first showroom in Boston.

In 1897, Paul's grandfather, Jerome Murphy, was just 16 years old when he started work at M. Steinert & Sons as a bookkeeper. "He used to come up with a sandwich during his lunch hour from taking classes at Bryant & Stratton Business School in Copley Square and watch the new Steinert building go up," says Paul.

By the early 1900s M. Steinert & Sons (and by this time there were seven sons) had as many as 42 stores throughout New England and New York along with two piano factories. The company prospered not only through its association with Steinway, but also because it diversified, selling not only used and new pianos, but player pianos, organs, and eventually radios and Victrolas.

The stock market crash and Depression brought the piano industry practically to a halt.

"The company was actually run by a group of disinterested Steinerts in that generation. So my grandfather bought the company in 1934 to keep his own job." To survive, the company needed to scale back and shuttered both factories and nearly all of its retail stores. However, Boston's Steinert Hall not only survived—it thrived.

Especially in the years before Symphony Hall opened in 1900, Steinert did much to create in Boston a taste and appreciation for good music. When Steinert Hall was built in 1896, the building also featured a (now-closed) beautifully designed—both aesthetically and acoustically—subterranean concert hall that hosted many fine musicians and ensembles of the day.

Today the six-floor Steinert Hall complex hums with activity. The street-level showroom is flooded with natural light from the large windows and has a wide range of new, used, and vintage Steinways (both uprights and grands) proudly on display. The store also sells the full line of Roland digital pianos for those with less space and smaller budgets (or reluctant piano-practicing children!). There is a dedicated performance space and studios for teaching piano—the store teaches 300 people, both kids and adults, every week. And two floors are dedicated to piano repair and restoration.

A lot of famous people practice at Steinert's before they go over to Symphony Hall: Lang Lang, Emanuel Axe, Diana Krall, and Herbie Hancock, to name just a few. Not too long ago, model Gisele Bundchen's publicist called to buy a piano for her Back Bay home, and "Gisele graciously took pictures with our guys who delivered it to her," Paul says.

Paul also recalls the time when composer John Williams asked Steinert's to send a loaner Steinway for his room at the Four Seasons. "He paid for the rental and returned it having written inside the lid in big letters 'John Williams' and the first few measures of the theme

to *Close Encounters of the Third Kind.* Soon after, a woman comes in and wants this type of piano. It is the only one we have and can't get another like it for six months. We tell her we have this piano and that it's been autographed by John Williams. 'That's a used piano; I can't buy that one,' says the woman."

Paul clearly loves the job. "It's a fun business. Getting to know the people who buy the pianos—that's what it is all about." Paul brought his son Brendan into the fold in 1999. "Now the fourth generation of Murphys are poised to take over the business after three generations of Steinerts," Paul says. It's quite a legacy.

NEW PARIS BAKERY

10 CYPRESS ST. • BROOKLINE, MA 02445

(617) 566-0926

World-Class Eclairs

Other than a move from Boston, and a series of ownership transfers within the founding Greek family, not much has changed for New Paris Bakery in the past 95 years or so. Located in Brookline since 1929, the New Paris Bakery continues to offer delectable pastries along with Old World charm. If you are looking to give in to temptation, this is the place.

As Marjorie Radlo, a longtime customer, puts it, "My grandfather Elizer Frank's (a man who spoke many languages, but whose first language was French) favorite place in Brookline was the New Paris Bakery. He took me there at least once a month when I was growing up. The éclairs are the best that I have ever had—including Paris!"

New Paris Bakery's ownership is a little complicated. Extended Greek families often are. Constantine, a Greek immigrant who learned his pastry-making skills in France, opened a bakery on Boston's Boylston Street (in the area of the present-day Prudential Tower) in 1919.

Constantine was the first cousin to current owner Roula Kappas's grandfather. Roula and her husband, James (Jimmy) Kappas, bought New Paris from the next generation owner—Roula's father's cousin—in 1988. For 24 years, until Jimmy's passing in 2012, Roula and Jimmy worked side by side in the bakery. "Jimmy was a person that was nice to work with," says Roula, who likes to remember. "I will tell you about the bakery. It brings me a lot of happiness when I talk about these things.

"I came to Boston from Greece with my parents in 1968 when I was 14 years old. We came here for opportunity. My father was a tailor. I knew Jimmy then. My parents eventually went back to Greece and I did too. But I came back to Boston. My mind was made up for my love, Jimmy. Everybody has a story. Everybody is a story."

Today the bakery still uses many of Constantine's original recipes, and the decor—from the ancient manual cash register to the simple display cases—hasn't changed in decades.

New Paris is a scratch bakery. Over the years the éclairs have won infinite fans. "Our éclairs bring people in," says Roula. At New Paris Bakery, the choux pastry is filled with pastry cream and topped with chocolate fondant icing. The éclairs are but one of Roula's daily offerings. Everything here is expertly turned out, from the classic napoleons to the eye-catching assortment of fresh fruit tarts to the dainty butter cookies to the almond paste candy. Asked if the bakery uses all butter, Roula is quick to reply. "All butter? Of course! Most places don't even break eggs; they buy frozen."

Roula and Jimmy never had children, but New Paris Bakery is still a family affair with Roula's nephew George working the counter. For Christmas, Roula will hire as many as a dozen people to help out.

"It's a unique store because it is old," she says. "You try to make it in a world that has changed a lot. Younger people come in here and say that their grandmother used to come here and they are almost crying. I love hearing stories like that." And Roula likes to tell her own story too.

NO NAME RESTAURANT

15½ FISH PIER ST. WEST • SOUTH BOSTON, MA 02210

(617) 338-7539 • NONAMERESTAURANT.COM

Last of the Old Waterfront Seafood Restaurants

*A*t the first light of day, to walk along Boston's Fish Pier is to experience the sights, sounds, and smell of a working fish pier: boats docked along the pier, lumpers unloading the haul, refrigerated trucks staged and ready. Opened in 1914, the Boston Fish Pier is one of the country's oldest fishing ports.

Jimmy Klidaras is No Name's general manager and the nephew of Katerina Contos, whose late husband, Nicholas, owned and operated No Name for more than four decades. Jimmy remembers well Boston Fish Pier's working-class tradition, not long gone. "It used to be like a small city down here. They used to have thousands of people working the docks. They had their own power plant, an icehouse, a bank, and their own bars and churches."

Nicholas's father, Iannis Contos, was a Greek immigrant who opened a restaurant on this same site at the Boston Fish Pier in 1917 called the Deluxe Diner. The diner was open only during the week, just for breakfast and lunch, and it catered to the men of the seaport: its fishermen and fishmongers. "It was an American diner, and back then we only served fish on Fridays," says Jimmy.

Nicholas Contos worked alongside his father at the diner throughout high school and college, eventually earning two master's degrees in business. Nicholas took over the diner in 1960, first offering dinner, then opening on the weekends and eventually converting the diner to a seafood restaurant. He also expanded the restaurant several times, adding a back room and second-floor dining space. Jimmy loves to

talk about No Name's history and his uncle. "My Uncle Nick, he was a good man; he taught me everything I know."

Some people just don't get No Name's—it is definitely a no-frills fish joint. The decor is vintage fish house—captain's chairs and anchors and life preservers are mounted on wood paneled walls—think the Krusty Krab from *SpongeBob*. Lucky you if you get one of the tables next to the windows with terrific views of the Boston Harbor and the planes taking off from and coming into Logan.

The waiters are salt-of-the-earth types who look as if they would be as comfortable working on a fishing vessel as serving seafood to the masses of locals and tourists who flock here for huge portions of inexpensive fried and broiled seafood.

No Name's seafood chowder is especially famous: milky and loaded with fish. It's what fishermen call "trim" chowder—made with what has been boned and trimmed that day. As Jimmy describes it, "We use haddock and cod, shrimp, chopped clams, clam juice, and a little evaporated milk. We don't use potatoes and we don't use flour."

And why "No Name"? Jimmy explains, "Over the years, we never put a sign out, we never gave the restaurant a name, so the customers gave it the name No Name. Uncle Nick said if it works, leave it alone."

Uncle Nick also told Jimmy to change with the times. "Like before we never had meat on the menu. We never sold lobster. Now we have salads and we even have pasta," says Jimmy. No Name also has free validated parking at its large lot next to the restaurant—not a small thing in the Seaport District, Boston's hottest new neighborhood.

Yet, despite the Seaport District's high-profile development, Boston's other legendary waterfront restaurants, Anthony's Pier 4 and Jimmy's Harborside, have closed. "Their kids didn't want it," says Jimmy. "We have family that will take over No Name. I'll be here for the next generation of the Contos family. I'll help them out."

PARKER'S RESTAURANT AT THE OMNI PARKER HOUSE HOTEL

60 SCHOOL ST. • BOSTON, MA 02108

(617) 227-8600 • OMNIPARKERHOUSE.COM

Hotel Dining Reminiscent of a Bygone Era

Spreading outward from the Boston Common, colonial Boston was founded on the meandering streets of present-day Downtown Crossing. Located directly on the Freedom Trail, and looming over the corner of Tremont and School Streets since 1855, the Omni Parker House Hotel is the longest continuously operating luxury hotel in the US. By the late 19th century, its restaurant became the most celebrated public dining room in Boston.

Another hotel, the Boylston, had been located on School Street in 1829, nearly 25 years before Harvey Parker, an entrepreneur and native of Maine, showed up to take on the challenge of building a new, "modernized" hotel, which he named Parker's.

The Parker House's neighbors were the next-door Tremont Theater, the Old Corner Bookstore just around the block, and eventually in 1865, Boston City Hall. From its inception Harvey Parker created a vision of the Parker House as a luxury hotel at the center of Boston's theatrical, literary, and political life.

In the mid- to late 19th century, Boston flourished as America's cultural cradle, especially in literature and the patronage of the arts. When Harvey Parker demolished the old Boylston he put up a hotel without equal in the city: a stone and brick Italianate structure five stories high with a white marble facade. The interior decor was just as splendid with a lobby that featured dark walnut paneling, burnished bronze fixtures, and overstuffed seating. Rooms had all the modern

conveniences of the time as well—including suites with private baths and both hot and cold running water.

Parker's large, handsome dining room with its hand-carved columns and crystal chandeliers was a model of Victorian opulence. And if these walls could talk! The Parker House still basks in its historic importance as a meeting place for some of Boston's great intellectuals of the 19th century.

From 1856 through 1920, Parker's was the site of the famed Saturday Club, an informal monthly round table where celebrated writers including Ralph Waldo Emerson, Nathaniel Hawthorne, and Henry Wadsworth Longfellow as well as scientists Louis Agassiz and Asa Gray gathered for drinking, dinner, and impassioned discussion. It is said that Longfellow penned the first draft of his poem "Paul Revere's Ride" here and that a visiting Charles Dickens held court giving his first American reading of *A Christmas Carol* to the group. The magazine the *Atlantic Monthly* was born at Parker's too.

From the beginning, the Parker House kitchen has been a breeding ground of culinary innovation. In the late 19th century, refined cooking had to be French, so Harvey Parker enlisted the help of the renowned French chef Sanzian to give Parker's restaurant cachet. In the 1850s and 1860s Parker's menu was exuberant and featured a lavish variety of items such as turtle soup, lobster salad in aspic, black-breast plover, tenderloin steaks with truffles, and charlotte russe. The 19th-century Parker House kitchen was also the birthplace of both the Boston cream pie—which isn't a pie at all, but a custard-filled, chocolate-topped sponge cake—and feather-light golden Parker House rolls. Legend has it, too, that the term "scrod," an acronym for "small cod received on dock," was first coined in the Parker House kitchens.

The Parker House kitchen is also notable for launching the culinary career of Emeril Lagasse, who worked here as a sous chef for two years early in his career. As a young man, Vietnamese Communist leader Ho Chi Minh apprenticed in Parker's kitchen as a baker's assistant. Another political activist, Malcolm Little, later known as Malcolm X, once worked at Parker's too—as a busboy in the 1940s.

As the Parker House prospered, Harvey Parker acquired additional property along School Street until the hotel eventually spanned nearly the entire city block. When Harvey Parker died in 1884 at the age of 79, the hotel's operation passed to Parker's business partners and eventually to various hotel management companies over the years. In 1927 the original Parker House Hotel was replaced with the present structure: a 14-story granite landmark building that retained much of the Parker House's unique Old World opulence. Currently, the Parker House is part of Omni Hotels & Resorts, and its 550 rooms and suites are known for their simple elegance and somewhat quirky sizes.

Regardless of ownership, Parker's restaurant has always featured a staff who take attentive to a whole new level. Lucky is the diner these days who is served by Gerry Mazzone, a career waiter who has been at the Parker House for more than 30 years, and has a dedicated following among the restaurant's regular customers.

Today Parker's cuisine may not be breaking new ground, which seems to please its loyal patrons and tourists just fine. They come for the experience of eating Boston cream pie and Parker House rolls in a legacy dining room that rivals any of the city's tourist sites.

PHILLIPS CANDY HOUSE

818 MORRISSEY BLVD. • BOSTON, MA 02122
(617) 282- 2090 • PHILLIPSCHOCOLATE.COM

Not Bad for a Company That Started in a Basement

Chipotle bourbon truffles and chocolate-covered bacon are fun to try—but the wholesome sweetness of classic creams and caramels enrobed in milk chocolate and dark chocolate never go out of style.

Phillips Candy House is a Boston institution and has been turning out small batches of its handmade confections for almost 90 years. The history of Phillips dates back to 1925, when Phillip and Constantina Strazzula began making wholesale chocolates in the basement kitchen of their Revere, Massachusetts, home. "My grandfather made the centers and my grandmother did the dipping," recalls Mary Ann Nagle, the third-generation owner of the shop.

It is still all in the family at Phillips Candy House. By 1930, the Strazzulas had perfected their recipes and candy-making techniques and had built quite a customer following. The Strazzulas opened the first Phillips candy store in Belmont, where Mary Ann Nagle's mother, Anna, learned the chocolate trade. By 1952, Anna, her husband, Joe Sammartino, and her three brothers moved Phillips Candy to its current location on Dorchester's Morrissey Boulevard—in a space that was once a clam shack. It was the era of roadside candy shops and people were traveling away from home for the first time, explains Mary Ann.

Boston's Dorchester neighborhood, in fact, has a 200-year old chocolate-making tradition. In 1765, John Hannon and James Baker established the first chocolate factory in America on the Neponset River in Dorchester Lower Mills. Baker's Chocolate, a purveyor of chocolate for the home baker, continued to operate here until 1965, when it was sold to General Foods.

In 2004 Phillips opened a second retail location at the South Shore Plaza in Braintree, which has proven very successful. The store's online presence is increasing as well. "We treat it as a small, third store. It's the way people shop today," says Mary Ann. The family enterprise, Phillips Hospitality Group, now involving a fourth generation, owns quite a bit of this corner of Dorchester's Pope's Hill neighborhood, including a Ramada Inn, a Comfort Inn, Boston Bowl, the Freeport Tavern, and Deadwood Cafe & Brewery.

Phillips Candy House is just that—a house. As you walk through the shop, the aroma of rich chocolate is intoxicating. All of Phillips candy production—that's 100,000 pounds of candy and chocolate— is hand molded, filled, wrapped, and packed from the modest kitchen in the back of the Dorchester headquarters.

"We have quite a number of old-time customers from South Boston and Dorchester, and newer people who come by and say that their aunt or mother used to shop at Phillips. So much of what we do here is traditional," says Mary Ann.

There really is too much to choose from. Of course there are elegantly prepackaged presentation boxes. The "theater box" of chocolates is a vestige from Phillips's early days. Mary Ann explains, "My grandparents enjoyed going to the opera. And years ago, when people used to go to the theater, they would take a little box of chocolates with them. It's still a great little gift for teachers or to drop on someone's desk."

You can also handpick your own specialty box from among the store's "serious chocolates"—the chocolate-covered creams and truffles displayed on open glass drawers are as pretty as they are delicate. Don't miss Phillips' much-loved turtles—made with milk or dark chocolate, cashews, almonds, or hazelnuts, and buttery caramel. Mary Ann buys only the highest quality chocolate and nuts. "Our caramel itself is a wonderful product which we make here. We use our family recipes, which are in a safe and under lock and key."

Tour the shop and you cannot help but be tempted. The sea salt–dusted caramels, slabs of dark chocolate almond bark, and Royal Hash—a chocolate-drenched smorgasbord of marshmallow, chopped nuts, and hazelnut butter—are geared to adult tastes. But the shelves are stocked too with child-friendly goodies, such as milk chocolate-dipped animal crackers, handmade peanut butter cups, and Oreo cookie chocolate bars. It seems that no matter your age, everyone becomes a kid in this candy store.

REGINA PIZZERIA

11½ THACHER ST. • BOSTON, MA 02113

(617) 227-0765 • REGINAPIZZERIA.COM

Nearly Unchanged for More Than 100 Years

*E*ven on the coldest winter day, there is a line stretching around the block of Regina Pizzeria, an institution in Boston's North End. Regina Pizzeria is so quaint and old-school appealing that people often comment that the pizzeria could pass for a movie set—which probably explains why it has done duty as a film location for Ben Affleck's *The Town* and the recent 100th anniversary Prince Spaghetti commercial.

Opened in 1926, Regina Pizzeria is the oldest pizzeria in Boston and has been owned by the Polcari family for three generations. According to Polcari family lore, the original owner had a "goomah," or mistress, and treated her like a lady, so he named his restaurant "Regina," Italian for "queen." Back in those days Polcari's was a small grocer, selling canned tomatoes, jug wine, and oil throughout the neighborhood including supplying Regina Restaurant. By 1946, the Regina Restaurant owed a lot of money to the Polcari family, so John Polcari Sr. took over the restaurant for his son Anthony, who was coming back from serving in North Africa during World War II.

Anthony Buccieri is the chief operating officer of Boston Restaurant Associates, the private company that today owns Regina Pizzeria in the North End along with the brand's 20-plus locations throughout New England. Anthony was born and raised in the North End and is related to the Polcari family by marriage; founder Anthony Polcari's wife, Mary, is his mother's sister.

Pies done the Regina way have crusts that are neither too thick nor too thin, and have a slightly charred bottom. Regina's goes to

great lengths to make sure their pizza is consistently superb throughout the company. The dough is made from an eight-decade-old original recipe and is hand-stretched; they don't use machines or even
rolling pins at Regina's. The aged, full-fat mozzarella on these pies is
made to Regina's specifications. "It's the good stuff," says Anthony.
Regina's signature sauce is bright, sweet, and light and is made especially for them. These brick-oven pies are then cooked to the customer's desired "doneness": lightly done, regular, or well done. Anthony
says, "Making Regina pizza takes a lot of know-hows."

As consistently great as Regina's pizza is, urban legend is that
pizza from the original North End restaurant is superior to that of
the chain's other outposts. What makes the pizzas in the North End
location special may be that they are baked in an 1888 gas-fired brick
oven (the oldest in the North End)—Regina's humble digs probably
help too.

Regina Pizzeria has largely refused to age with time but it has
tons of character and charm. The crowded, noisy dining room has
seating for just 60 patrons. The wood booths are more than 50 years
old and have been put
together piecemeal. The
walls are painted a Tuscan
yellow and have a large
number of celebrity photographs including Leonardo
DiCaprio and Rene Russo.
The small, cluttered bar is
in the front and decorated
with the department insig-
nia of some of the local
firefighters and policemen
who are frequent custom-
ers. And although once
famous as much for its
brusque waitresses as its
pies, these days service is
much more welcoming—
almost friendly.

Regina's menu is simple; pizza, beer, wine, and soda. According to Anthony, the most popular pies are cheese, pepperoni, and its Giambotta, or kitchen sink: pepperoni, sausage, salami, mushrooms, onions, and peppers. Some days they can crank out as many as 1,000 pies from the ancient oven. Anthony says that Regina's customers run the gamut from locals coming in after a game at the Boston Garden to city hall workers on their lunch hour to tourists who hear about Regina through Yelp and Trip Advisor.

"Everyone that comes here doesn't want us to change anything," according to Anthony. "But you know what? We have changed, little by little. We went to credit cards 20 years ago. The customers asked for TVs over the bar and now they want Wi-Fi too. But we haven't changed the food. We don't need to."

RON'S GOURMET ICE CREAM AND 20TH CENTURY BOWLING LANES

1231 HYDE PARK AVE. • BOSTON, MA 02136

(617) 364-5274 • RONSICECREAM.COM

Ice Cream and Candlepins:
A Perfect Excuse for an Outing

There is no better spot than this old-school candlepin joint and ice cream shop for throwback awesomeness. Ron's is a local institution that bridges generations in the close-knit community

of Hyde Park, Boston's southernmost neighborhood. Boston's residency requirement is alive and well here. The tree-lined streets and affordable single-family homes make Hyde Park a favorite place for the city's teachers, firefighters, and police officers to raise a family.

Located next to the Hyde Park police station, the shop has a decor that is charmingly outdated, with wood-paneled walls that display Ron's current candlepin league team photos and numerous best ice cream awards from both national (*Good Morning America*) and local (*Boston Magazine*) media.

Ron's ice cream really is terrific. Made on-site, this ice cream has perfect richness and density and is packed with flavor. But half the fun of visiting Ron's is the wholesome pleasure of candlepin bowling—New England's quirky variation of tenpin bowling.

Invented in Worcester in 1880, candlepin bowling features narrower pins and small, no-hole balls. The candlepin balls are easy for kids to handle. But don't be deceived; candlepin bowling is wicked hard—and New Englanders take candlepin bowling very seriously.

Over six decades Ron's has changed with the times. Current owner Ron Covitz's father, Julius, bought the ten-lane candlepin bowling alley in 1952. "My grandfather drove in from Worcester during a snowstorm to lend my father the money to buy the building," says Ron. "Back then, we didn't have automatic pin setters, we had pin boys to reset the pins." By the late 1950s, Julius had expanded the business and put in a pool hall downstairs. In 1961, Paul Newman and Jackie Gleason starred in *The Hustler.* "Pool was hot back then," remembers Ron. But by the 1970s pool halls were in decline.

After spending a short time in the service, Ron came to work for his father. "As he started not to feel well, I took over more of the responsibilities." When Julius passed away in 1976, Ron closed the pool hall. "I was 29 at the time. I knew that ten lanes of bowling wasn't enough, but I didn't know how to grow the business."

By 1979 Ron had begun to diversify by making soft-serve ice cream at the bowling alley. At the time, Hood Dairy was Ron's supplier. The story of Ron's foray into gourmet ice cream–making is accidental. Ron explains, "They sent me the wrong ice cream mix and the vice president of Hood came down. On the way out the front door he said, 'Ronnie, if you find a good location, I think that making hard gourmet ice cream could be the wave of the future.'"

Ron's ice cream is 14 percent butterfat, made with the best flavorings in a low overrun batch freezer. "I was able to successfully make ice cream in a bowling alley, even though no one believed that I could," says Ron with a smile.

In 1998 Ron's expanded by opening another ice cream shop in the nearby town of Dedham. Running the business is a full-time family affair for the Covitzes. Ron's wife, Pat, has decorated the store's ice cream cakes for the past 26 years. They are much in demand—Ron's hosts as many as seven children's birthday parties on the weekends. Throughout their youth, each of Ron and Pat's three children worked in the store. Today their son Jay works as the store's general manager and is in charge of making most of the store's ice cream. There are more than 30 flavors to choose from and among the store's most popular are the Oreo, caramel fudge brownie, rum raisin, and Grapenut. Ron says, "More than anything else we love being a place where families come to be together and have a good time."

RUBIN'S KOSHER RESTAURANT

500 HARVARD ST. • BROOKLINE, MA 02446

(617) 731-8787 • RUBINSBOSTON.COM

Brookline's Kosher Jewish Deli: Last of a Dying Breed

Slip into a red vinyl booth at this traditional Old World deli, where it's impossible during the busy lunch hour not to eavesdrop on your neighbor's conversation. "I like to say this is the kosher

Cheers, where everyone knows your name," says Allen Gellerman, owner of Rubin's in Brookline.

Rubin's is Boston's only remaining kosher deli. It specializes in unadulterated Jewish soul food—this is the kind of place where you can still get stuffed cabbage, smoked fish, and a bowl of matzo ball soup. The meats, including aromatic corned beef and peppery pastrami—staples at any self-respecting deli—are hand-carved and piled high between slices of rye bread and served with half sour pickles. Dr. Brown's cream soda, a deli staple, is the drink of choice.

Rubin's is located on Brookline's Harvard Street, the epicenter of the region's Jewish community, a few doors down from a Jewish butcher and across the street from a Judaica bookstore. Like other kosher businesses, Rubin's is closed on Friday afternoon and all day Saturday—and consequently it's a madhouse from open to close on Sunday.

The Grupp family established Rubin's in 1928, owning the deli through four generations. In 1997, Allen bought Rubin's. "I worked in a kosher meat market with my uncles and I was looking for a business.

Rubin's was for sale and already established. You can't find better than that," he declares.

It used to be that Rubin's catered to an older crowd. According to Allen, the average age of Rubin's customers is now in the mid-40s. Despite its size, the Boston metropolitan area has surprisingly few kosher dining options; some of Rubin's customers come in three or four times a week.

For Rubin's many regulars, there is no lack of variety from the mega menu. Breakfast all day features latkes, challah french toast, and lox bagel boards with all the usual fixings. "Over the years, we've changed the menu; it is more upscale, more contemporary," says Allen. The dinner menu offers upgraded Yiddish classics—seared beef tongue with portobello mushrooms on grilled challah crostini, barley and mushroom pilaf, and honey balsamic grilled lamb chops. "We sell a lot of salmon at dinner. People are more diet conscious now," says Allen.

Deli aficionados trek to Rubin's from all over, including visitors from Europe, South Africa, Australia, and Israel. Although outside of New England, Rubin's biggest clientele is from New York. "They appreciate this place; we don't give them attitude and we are less expensive," Allen explains. Many of Boston's hotels and universities depend on Rubin's to deliver kosher meals to their guests. Allen recalls that his biggest order ever was supplying kosher meals for the 2004 Democratic National Convention at the Boston Garden.

Rubin's is a deli holdout, but hanging on. Allen is revamping his website, sprucing up the restaurant's decor with newly framed vintage photographs, and has recently installed an outdoor patio for alfresco dining.

Allen is the father of a son and daughter, both attending college. "My kids help when they are home for breaks, but they don't have any interest in the business. You work hard, day and night, in the restaurant business to make sure that your kids have a future better than your own. But I don't know what's next for Rubin's."

SALUMERIA ITALIANA

151 RICHMOND ST. • BOSTON, MA 02109

(617) 523-8743 • SALUMERIAITALIANA.COM

The Tastes of Italy

Boston's North End still bleeds green, white, and red. And food is taken rather seriously in the neighborhood. You'll be lured into Salumeria Italiana by the bread stacked in baskets in the front window. And when you step into the shop you will be overcome

by the smells: imported cured salami, pungent oil-soaked olives, and freshly grated Asiago cheese.

This is also the place to get your extra-virgin olive oil and balsamic vinegar fix. Look for regional oils from all over Italy: Frantoia from Sicily, Ranieri from Liguria, and white truffle oil from Umbria. Then treat yourself to true *aceto balsamico*: aged in casks with a perfect balance of sweet and sour. Among Salumeria Italiana's offerings is an eight-year-old artisanal-style balsamic from 400-year-producer Giusti.

Americans may now know the difference between prosciutto and pancetta, and can even buy them at their local grocery store. Salumeria Italiana excels in offering high-quality Italian ingredients that are still hard to find: jars of salt-packed anchovies, *mostarda* (a mustard-flavored fruit compote), *n'duja* (a spicy, spreadable salami pâté), and an arcane collection of Italian honey. If you need a fanciful pasta shape like *strozzapreti* (priest stranglers) or the stamped coin-shaped discs known as *croxetti*, this is your place. The store also stocks ravioli forms, Bialetti replacement gaskets, and (very useful) stainless steel oil pourers.

Behind the counter, owner Guy Martignetti greets customers in English (or if need be, Italian). He makes frequent trips to Italy, attending food trade shows and then going off the beaten path to find new products. Says Guy, "We don't stock many prepared foods. We are more hard-core. You have to know the essentials of Italian cooking. You have to know how to cook."

Although the redbrick Freedom Trail brings waves of people down Salem Street on their way to the Paul Revere House, Guy says that the store doesn't get a whole lot of business from tourists. Most of the shop's customers are North End residents (or former residents) and their far-flung relatives and children who come back on the weekend to shop for authentic Italian food.

It was the desire for a taste of home that created Salumeria Italiana back in 1962. "When I was born, the shop was born," says Guy. "My mother had just come to America. The things that my mother was used to in Italy were not available, so she needed my dad to step up to the plate."

Guy's father, Erminio, immigrated to the US from the Campania region of Italy in the 1950s to join the Martignetti family's successful

wine and grocery store operation. Striking out on his own, Erminio opened Salumeria Italiana so that his wife could make Italian food. By 1982 Erminio was able to purchase the store's building as well. For more than five decades, the shop has thrived with Guy taking over the business full-time about 20 years ago. "I have never been too far from the shop. When I was little, the shop was my playground. I have quit about 100 times. But they always leave a spot for you to come back to," he says.

SANTARPIO'S PIZZA

111 CHELSEA ST. • EAST BOSTON, MA 02128

(617) 567-9871 • SANTARPIOSPIZZA.COM

No-Frills Pizza Parlor

This charmingly shabby East Boston landmark requires a trek through the Callahan Tunnel but buzzes with both locals and tourists (it's also on the way to Logan, making it a very popular detour for travelers coming to and from the airport). And despite countless national and local accolades for its pizza, Santarpio's, which East Boston residents affectionately call "Tarp's," is essentially still a neighborhood pizzeria that hasn't changed much over time.

The atmosphere is dark and divey; the decor is frozen in an apparent 1960s redo with photos of boxing greats on the battered walls, scratched wooden booths, and Frank Sinatra on the jukebox. These thin-crust pies are traditional yet anything but ordinary—the housemade sausage and fresh-cut garlic pizza is the stuff of legend.

Santarpio's prices are more than reasonable—a carafe of wine at Santarpio's is about the same price as a glass of wine downtown—which means the dining room is always crowded and busy. Be prepared to wait. And wait. If you are impatient, there is always take-out—call ahead, go around to the back door, and walk into the kitchen for pick-up. That there are no desserts and payment is cash only (there's an ATM on-site) shouldn't surprise.

Opened in 1903 as a bread bakery by Italian immigrant Francisco Santarpio, this is one of the neighborhood's oldest businesses. Today Santarpio's still makes bread from the same recipe. A hunk of bread and cherry peppers accompanies all of Santarpio's barbecue items: grilled lamb, steak tips, or homemade sausage. "It's all very rustic," says Joia Santarpio, fourth-generation owner (along with her

brothers Frank and Joe and sister Carla) and the youngest of the Santarpio siblings.

Francisco's son Joseph was an athlete. "When he was young, my grandfather was a professional baseball prospect. But my great-grandfather told him he couldn't just play ball, he had to bake the bread." Joseph eventually came around, taking over Santarpio's from his father. After Prohibition, Joseph expanded the business to include a bar, Santarpio's Cafe, which became a center for East Boston's Italian immigrant community. Joia explains, "They would have a lot of drunk guys hanging around, so my grandfather started feeding them whatever he was making. Some days it was tripe, other days lamb or macaroni. That's what they would serve for lunch at the bar."

Pizza was added to Santarpio's menu relatively recently—in the 1940s. Most of the credit for Santarpio's pizza belongs to Joia's great-uncle, Joe Timpone. Joe was a plasterer by day. By night, he would come to the restaurant and make pizza. The architecture of Joe's pizza pie making was unique for the time: on top of the crust he would first put the toppings, then the tomato sauce, and finally the cheese.

Santarpio's pizza-making method hasn't changed in nearly 70 years, and why should it? "I don't think anyone ever questioned Joe," says Joia. "We still make our pizzas his way, and it works." Joseph's son Frank took over Santarpio's in 1966. "My dad is responsible for converting the bar into a pizzeria, making Santarpio's the success that it is today," says Joia. "He and my mom are retired, but they come by to help and to socialize."

Joia says that business has been very good. "We've been very fortunate with our location," she says. "The tunnel and airport weren't here when we acquired the building. We also have a lot of regulars that keep coming back and bring their children." In 2010 the family opened a second location in Peabody, where the fifth generation of Santarpios is learning how to run the family's restaurants. Joia says with a laugh, "The pizza business sucks you in."

SOUTH STREET DINER

178 KNEELAND ST. • BOSTON, MA 02111
(617) 350-0028 • DINERBOSTON.COM

Boston's Late-Night Refuge 24/7

S outh Street is a true diner—lots of chrome, Formica, and neon— with doors that are always open and not a bit of manufactured nostalgia. As far back as the 1930s there was a Worcester Lunch Car Company diner on this site. In 1943, two brothers, returning from World War II, built the current brick and ribbed stainless steel structure on the premises to the exact size of its tiny sliver of a corner city lot across from South Station.

In those days it was known as the Blue Diner, serving affordable meals fast to Leather District factory workers on the late-night shift. Today, beneath the giant coffee cup on its roof, South Street Diner is a bona-fide landmark to clubgoers looking for food that will cure a hangover and for the city's assorted night owls (taxicab drivers and hospital workers among them) who come in for blue-plate specials and the fading tradition of a bottomless cup of coffee.

South Street Diner is itself a local celebrity and through the years has been featured in countless films, including *21* (2008) with Kevin Spacey. The diner has also been the subject of the 2012 award-winning documentary *24 Hours at the South Street Diner*.

Sol Sidell has been running the show here since 1997, giving the diner a limited restoration, a menu upgrade, and renaming it the South Street Diner soon after buying it. He modestly refers to himself as an "egg-flipper," but he is considered one of the city's leading restaurant owners. "When I bought the diner, we started with six employees and 600 customers a week," Sol recalls. "Now we have 40 employees and 600 customers in an average night."

Sol has been in the restaurant business since he was a kid, first working as a dishwasher. "I asked my mother for a raise in my allowance and she told me to find a job," Sol says. Over the years Sol worked his way up in the food industry; first as a pizza maker, eventually owning several hot dog stands before working as a corporate opener for Hyatt Hotels and Palm Steak restaurants. In 2009, Sol and the South Street Diner faced the Boston Licensing Board after noise complaints by neighbors. Thanks to Sol's tenacity and lots of customer love, he won.

Boston goes to bed early and South Street is always busiest around 2 a.m., after last call, when Boston's bars close. It's a killer scene. On most weekend nights, there will be a line of more than 100 people outside. And by the wee hours of the morning, the restaurant becomes the after-party place for every bartender, cocktail waitress, and doorman in the city. But nobody seems to mind the wait.

South Street offers breakfast, lunch, and dinner along with a wine/ beer license. Breakfast is served all day and features eggs, three-egg omelets (all eggs are served with toast and hash browns), pancakes, and french toast along with all the sides: bacon, sausage, ham, or corned beef hash. For lunch and dinner, South Street serves homey, simply executed food. Favorites on the menu include their hamburgers, grilled cheese sandwiches, and steak tip dinner. Order a malted egg cream—the milky, seltzer-sweet taste will transport you back to the 1950s. A slice of scratch-made blueberry or apple pie rounds out the bygone experience.

Everyone is on equal footing here. Sol says his customers are "any and all," from the homeless guy on the corner to celebrities to the most anonymous college student to international tourists to South Boston home-grown. The quirky staff can be brusque—at least until they get to know you. Regulars tend to sit elbow-to-elbow on the counter stools facing the grill. And everybody loves the inviting deep four-person booths along the front windows.

The area has changed a lot, from a seedy neighborhood to a cyber-district, a transportation mecca, and now a residential hub of the city. At the South Street Diner, portions are large, prices are low, and the crowd is always cool. As Sol puts it, "There are 30 colleges and half a million students within a five-mile radius of downtown. At 2:30 in the morning it's me and Mum, and Mum don't want to cook it."

STERLINGWEAR OF BOSTON

175 WILLIAM F. MCCLELLAN HWY. • EAST BOSTON, MA 02128
(617) 567-2100 • STERLINGWEAROFBOSTON.COM

Clothing Proudly Manufactured
in Massachusetts

Sterlingwear of Boston has been manufacturing the official US Navy peacoat since the 1960s. In the mid-1980s Sterlingwear began selling peacoats to the civilian market—mostly through army-navy stores. Today, Sterlingwear offers a broad range of nearly 200 styles: peacoats, trench coats, and even high-fashion outerwear

for the retail market. But the peacoat remains the company's best-selling jacket. It never goes out of style.

A family-owned and -operated union shop, Sterlingwear employs nearly 300 workers at its East Boston factory. Sterlingwear was founded in 1965 by first-generation American Frank Fredella as Viking Clothing, a cut and sew contractor. The Fredella story is a classic American immigrant tale of working hard, realizing a dream, and passing the business on to the next generation.

In the 1920s Lorenzo Fredella, then just 16 years old, came to America from Italy. Lorenzo's cousins had a clothing factory in New York where he worked various jobs: sweeping, hauling, and operating a sewing machine. Eventually Lorenzo became a supervisor and when the factory moved to Massachusetts, Lorenzo relocated as well. In his mid-twenties Lorenzo married; in time he and his wife, Jenny, would have five children.

During the late 1920s Lorenzo was employed at East Boston's Picariello and Singer, at the time one of the country's leading clothing manufacturers. Lorenzo's son Frank joined the company at the age of 16, working as a part-time designer and pattern maker while attending high school. In due course, Frank worked his way up the ranks at the factory learning all aspects of the business while attending

Boston University in the evenings. During this time period, Frank left Picariello and Singer to serve two years with the US Army in the Korean War. After returning from Korea, Frank married and he and his wife, Jo, had two children. Frank went back to work at Picariello and Singer and with persistence, earned his business degree from Boston University in 1961.

In 1965 Frank urged Lorenzo to go into business for himself. "My brother Anthony (an attorney) and I convinced him that it was time and so we both left the company. It was the time to get my father's dream going."

Frank's company was truly a very small business—35 rented machines in a leased building in Cambridge—which formed the basis of Viking Clothing. By 1967, at the height of the Vietnam War, Viking was asked by the US government to set aside some of their production to make Army overcoats and Navy peacoats. Viking's first armed forces contract helped to accelerate the growth of the fledgling company. Viking changed its name to Viking Military (Vi-Mil) and moved to a bigger factory—ironically Picariello and Singer's former facility, which had closed in the early 1970s.

By the early 1980s, there was a decline in government contracts and Vi-Mil decided to diversify by purchasing Sterlingwear, a manufacturer of raincoats. "Since we were making raincoats for the government, we felt it was a good way to get into the commercial market and still make the items that we were familiar with producing," says Frank. "They already had a name in industry, so we changed our name to Sterlingwear."

Today, 75 percent of Sterlingwear's production is government contract outerwear and uniforms. But the company has worked hard to diversify in the fashion apparel industry. Today Sterlingwear can be found in specialty stores and boutiques throughout the country. Sterlingwear also produces peacoats in partnership with L.L. Bean. In 2009 the decision was made open Sterlingwear retail stores. The company's East Boston store is adjacent to the factory where the whir of sewing machines and the hiss of industrial steam irons are just beyond the door. Here, the inventory of coats is deep, as are the discounts.

"Made in America" is not a new mantra at Sterlingwear; the company produces 100 percent domestically and has since its inception.

Sterlingwear's employees represent many ethnicities: the low murmur of Italian, Russian, Chinese, and Spanish can be heard on the factory floor. Sterlingwear treats its employees like family, even naming its coat styles for its employees. In 2005, when it was necessary to relocate the company to a larger facility, Frank insisted that the company remain in East Boston so that he wouldn't displace or lose any of his workers. Sterlingwear stayed in East Boston, moved 1 mile to its current location—and retained its entire workforce.

Frank continues his role as president and CEO of Sterlingwear. And although well past "retirement" age, he is known to walk the factory floor every day. Today Sterlingwear's management is in its third generation of leadership with Frank's son Larry and daughter Gina, along with Frank's nephew David (Anthony's son), continuing the tradition of the family business and made-in-America manufacturing.

SULLIVAN'S

2080 WILLIAM J. DAY BLVD. • BOSTON, MA 02127

(617) 268-5685 • SULLIVANSCASTLEISLAND.COM

After More Than Six Decades, the Lines Still Have Not Gone Away

Everyone thinks they know Southie. Thanks to Hollywood (and Matt and Ben), films like *Good Will Hunting, The Departed, Gone Baby Gone,* and *The Town* seem to have defined South Boston to the outside world as a criminal movie set populated primarily by petty thieves and the Irish mob.

The real Southie—a close-knit working-class neighborhood of Boston—is quite different. However, the area really does bleed green—the neighborhood accent is "r-less" with a touch of brogue, the streets are almost entirely lined with wooden triple-deckers, and there are an inordinate number of pubs up and down West Broadway. You'll find, too, that Southie natives walk Castle Island and afterward, often get something to eat at Sullivan's.

Located on South Boston's Pleasure Bay, Sullivan's, or "Sullies," is a takeout-only food stand that sits in the shadow of Castle Island's Fort Independence, the granite pentagon-shaped fortification that has guarded Boston's Inner Harbor since 1851. Castle Island is a misnomer—it's no longer an island, as it was connected to the mainland by landfill in the early 1900s. Today it is a 22-acre state park that includes not only Fort Independence (which offers a schedule of historic tours Memorial Day weekend through Columbus Day) but also Carson Beach, a playground, a fishing pier, and a looping 2-mile paved walking path.

The menu at Sullivan's seems to summon a salty sea breeze. Hungry locals happily brave epic lines for fried seafood, hot dogs, and ice

cream at this Boston landmark, unchanged in decades (except for the nifty solar panels on the roof). It's a counter-only operation, but there are a few picnic tables outside if you don't feel like walking along the causeway to the beach just yet. Sullivan's certainly makes the most of its setting. The view of the harbor, the low roar of planes landing at and taking off from nearby Logan Airport, and even the stalker seagulls are iconic Boston.

Sullivan's is a third-generation family business, now owned and managed by Brendan Sullivan, who "officially" began working here in 1985 but remembers sweeping the restaurant floor when he was just 12. Brendan's grandfather, Dan Sullivan Sr., opened an aluminum concession stand with a drop-down window on Castle Island in 1951, selling hot dogs for 15 cents each.

By 1963 Sullivan's had outgrown the space and replaced it with a cinder-block building. In 1976 Brendan's father, Dan Sullivan Jr., took over and by 1989 constructed the current brick building, which was designed to mimic the 1807 Commandant's house that once stood here. Sullivan's owns the building but has a long-term lease from the

Massachusetts Department of Conservation and Recreation. Asked about the future of Sullivan's, Brendan says, "I have three young boys. Hopefully, someday one of them will want it."

According to Brendan, Sullivan's top seller is its hot dogs. Known locally as "snap dogs," the slightly crunchy yet juicy Kayem brand beef and pork franks are grilled up with little ceremony and served in a lightly toasted bun. Most regulars order their hot dogs "all-around," with mustard, relish, and onion. Sullivan's is also known for its seafood including fried cod and fried clam bellies, lobster rolls, clam chowder, and fish sandwiches along with fried onion rings and crinkle-cut fries. Says Brendan, "Our name alone stands for good food at low prices. We are a volume restaurant and we need beautiful weather; otherwise no one comes."

So who comes? "Basically everyone from all over the city," says Brendan. "Locals from South Boston and Dorchester, businesspeople from downtown for lunch, college and high school kids in the afternoon, mothers with strollers in the mornings." And of course, Sullivan's gets all the local politicians like Billy Bulger (former state Senate president and brother of notorious mobster Whitey Bulger), former Boston mayor Ray Flynn, and US Senator Elizabeth Warren. Last summer Vice President Joe Biden stopped in too.

Sullivan's is more than New England summertime fare. It holds a special place in the hearts of South Boston residents who come to enjoy the sunset, a stroll around Pleasure Bay's "Sugar Bowl," and the notion (even if untrue) that there is nowhere else you need to be.

SYRIAN GROCERY IMPORTING CO.

270 SHAWMUT AVE. • BOSTON, MA 02118

(617) 426-1458

A Middle East Market Gone Gourmet

In a neighborhood that has endured enormous changes, Syrian Grocery Importing remains authentic. Walk inside the cramped 1,000-square-foot shop and you're instantly transported: worn wooden floors that slope, and painted turquoise shelves stocked with nuts, dried fruits, lentils, chickpeas, and grains sold in bulk. And the spices! The heady aroma of Turkish coffee and cardamom is a wonderful combination.

From the early 1940s until the 1970s, Boston's South End neighborhood was home to a vibrant Syrian, Lebanese, and Greek community. The shabby brick storefront of the Syrian Grocery Importing Company has been a fixture in the neighborhood for more than 70 years despite years of gentrification, which has pushed out most of the community's remaining Middle East residents.

Brothers Montgomery, Ramon, and Joseph Mansour own Syrian Grocery Importing Company, which was bought in 1967 by their father, Maurice Mansour. The Mansours have deep roots in the neighborhood. Their mother, Margaret, a Lebanese-American, was born down the street at 70 Shawmut Ave. In 1952, while visiting relatives in Lebanon, Margaret met Maurice and soon after, Maurice immigrated to Boston.

At the time, Syrian Grocery Importing was an established business, originally founded in the 1940s by two Syrian immigrants in the vicinity of Hudson and Tyler Streets, in what is now Boston's Chinatown neighborhood. Boston's first wave of Syrian immigrants settled in Chinatown's South Cove area. Joseph explains, "As the community

was getting bigger, they needed more space, so they came out this way, to the South End, and the store followed the community."

In Lebanon Maurice was a firearms maker by trade. In Boston he worked rebuilding electric motors for Holtzer-Cabot Electric Company in Jamaica Plain. "My father was self-educated," says Joseph. "But he wanted to work in a way that allowed him to keep touch with the Lebanese community. He tried to buy the grocery store in 1964 but the deal fell through. He had another opportunity to buy it in 1967 when the original owner decided to put it on the market after his oldest son had died in Vietnam." In 1975 Maurice was able to buy the 1870s building, which includes the store's retail space and three apartments on the upper floors. "My father wanted to secure the business by owning the building. That was important to him," says Joseph. The family also owns the deserted (pun intended) Sahara Syrian restaurant down the street.

How does Joseph feel about the future of the store? "Business is more difficult than it used to be, because there are more stores trying to sell the same things. In the old days, my father sold strictly

Middle Eastern groceries. He didn't carry the variety that we do, but he didn't need to either. There was no Trader Joe's, no Whole Foods. Now Middle Eastern food has become mainstream."

In the old days, the store was a gathering place for the Syrian/Lebanese community. A good number of fellow immigrants still return to stock up on pantry staples like the store's own blend of Arabic allspice, Aleppo pepper flakes, bulgur, and hard-to-find red lentils. But now customers include a growing number of adventurous home chefs as well as people who just enjoy ethnic cuisines. "I can sort of tell right away when people are making a new recipe. Preserved lemons are popular and anything with figs," says Joseph. Nearby Tremont Street—home to Mistral, The Butcher Shop, and Coppa—is often referred to as "Restaurant Row." "This is a very gourmet area," says Joseph.

Long ago, Syrian Importing gave up the pretense of being just a Middle Eastern grocery store. Today it is stocked with unique food finds from around the world—not only the Middle Eastern goods like pomegranate molasses, olives and feta cheese, and a massive selection of olive oil, but products from Europe and South Asia too. The store stocks jams and chocolates from France and England, simmer sauces and tamarind from India, and peanut oil from Hong Kong. The hookah water pipes are popular with the college crowd, and north African tagine cooking vessels and stainless steel kebab skewers appeal to foodies. Syrian Importing is always worth a trip simply to stock your spice rack; the bonus is that you are sure to find something you've never heard of when you visit.

THE TAJ BOSTON

15 ARLINGTON ST. • BOSTON, MA 02116

(617) 598-5220 • TAJHOTELS.COM/TAJBOSTON

Tea at the Taj Boston: Steeped in History

*B*oston knows a little something about having a tea party. After all, it was on a frigid December night in 1773 that a mob of colonists tossed 340 chests of tea into Boston Harbor to protest a British tax on tea. In fact, in Boston it was actually considered unpatriotic to drink tea during the American Revolutionary War years. Boston's complicated relationship with tea notwithstanding, the tradition of an English-style afternoon tea lives on at the Taj Boston.

The Taj Boston has always been considered one of the city's most iconic hotels. From its unparalleled location—at the corner of fashionable Newbury Street and across from the Boston Public Garden—to its reputation for old-school luxury (complimentary overnight shoeshine!), the hotel has always attracted guests of wealth, power, and taste, including Elizabeth Taylor, Howard Hughes, and Winston Churchill. Lots of current celebrities, politicians, and dignitaries still come through these doors, but the Taj Boston is famed as well for its discretion. So even today, if you do sit at the bar, you never know who you will run into.

Originally the Boston Ritz Carlton, when the 17-story, 270-room hotel opened in 1927 it was the epitome of formal luxury and the hotel of choice for Boston society. And although Bostonians were quick to raise their eyebrows when India-based Taj Hotels Resorts and Palaces took over in 2007, the brand has managed to inject a touch of India while embracing both the building's history and traditions. Brian Macaluso, Taj Boston's director of sales and marketing, says, "Guests can be confident that if and when we make any changes, the traditions of Boston will always be here. It's all in keeping with what the Taj has always done."

Thankfully some things never change. Whether tea at the Taj or tea at the Ritz, generations of Boston mothers, daughters, and granddaughters have come to the elegant second-floor French Room to celebrate a birthday, attend a bridal shower, or enjoy a girls' day out in the city. Afternoon tea unfolds on Saturday and Sunday afternoons (reservations are recommended) in the elegant, light-filled salon, which features crystal chandeliers, comfortable chairs, and original artwork. The tea service itself is as gracious as the setting: classic three-tiered silver trays replete with dainty cucumber sandwiches, smoked salmon canapés, warm currant scones with clotted cream, and an assortment of pastries varied enough to satisfy any sweet tooth. A porcelain pot of tea is delivered with a graceful flourish; you can choose from a vast selection of 20 types including a standard Darjeeling and estate-grade oolong blends.

The serenade of a harpist or violinist adds to the ambience—and tables are far enough apart for intimate conversation. And you will feel well looked after as the attentive staff attends to every detail of the tea service—including pouring your tea through a tea strainer lest any stray leaves find a way into your cup.

Although this is traditionally the preserve of women, guys are welcome for afternoon tea at the Taj Boston too. Gone are the days when wearing a jacket and tie were de rigueur. "It's still a formal tea, but going along with the times, we want it to be a little more casual," Brian says.

Boston will be forever linked to tea. Afternoon tea at the Taj Boston is one of the city's enduring rituals and a not-to-be-missed experience that will leave you feeling both pampered and relaxed. A long early evening walk through the Public Garden and Boston Common afterward is not a bad idea either.

UNION OYSTER HOUSE

41 UNION ST. • BOSTON, MA 02108
(617) 227-2750 • UNIONOYSTERHOUSE.COM

Almost Two Centuries of Dining History

In a rambling 18th-century brick structure with low ceilings, original high-back wood stalls, and wide-plank floors, your meal will be as Bostonian as it gets when you dine at the Union Oyster House, which opened as an oyster house and bar in 1826 and is considered the country's oldest continually operating restaurant.

If you can, sit at the original mahogany oyster bar set in the restaurant's front window. Somehow, freshly shucked oysters always

taste better at the bar. It's still a genuine Boston experience—you may even feel the ghostly presence of oyster lovers past. The statesman and famed orator Daniel Webster was a regular customer. "He would have a brandy and water with each plate of oysters and it is said that he never had less than six plates at a time," says longtime general manager Jim Malinn. Today oysters on the half shell are still one of the restaurant's most popular menu items; the restaurant sells 60,000 plates of oysters in a typical year.

Not just another local institution, the Union Oyster House, both the building and the business, have been designated a National Historic Landmark. The Union Oyster House is located directly on the Freedom Trail on the Blackstone block, one of the oldest parts of the city—a cobblestone alley that has largely been unaltered since the 18th century.

The building itself was already more than 100 years old when the Atwood and Bacon Oyster House opened here. Jim says, "We had some architectural historians assess the building and they think the original structure dates from 1716 to 1718." Over its 300 years, the building has had many different uses. In 1742, it was a fancy dress shop known as "At the Sign of the Cornfields." From 1771 to 1775, the second floor of the building housed the print shop of Isaiah Thomas, who published the *Massachusetts Spy,* the most widely read and influential colonial newspaper of the day. And in 1796 the exiled future (and final) king of France, Louis Philippe, lived in the building's second-floor rooms for several months tutoring the fine young ladies of Boston in French.

For well over 80 years, the Atwood family ran the restaurant as a simple oyster and ale house. In 1913 the Atwoods sold the restaurant to the Fitzgerald family, who changed the name to the Union Oyster House. The Greaves brothers bought the restaurant in 1940 and in 1970 they sold the business to the Milano family; brother Joe and sister Mary Ann Milano Picardi run it to this day, having greatly expanded the restaurant over the years by purchasing adjacent buildings.

Besides raw oysters, Daniel Webster would recognize the fried clams and scallops still on the menu. Today's Union Oyster House excels at the usual roster of traditional New England regional dishes: clam chowder, Boston baked beans, broiled cod, boiled lobster, and fish and chips, along with steaks and chops. You may also want to

have the house draft; the Sam Adams Union Oyster House Colonial Ale is brewed especially for the restaurant.

In modern times, the Union Oyster House has been frequented by a slew of prominent names, none more famous than John F. Kennedy, who dined almost weekly at the Union Oyster House during the early years of his political career when he represented Massachusetts—first as a congressman and then a senator—in Washington, DC. His favorite seat was booth number 18 on the second floor—you can call ahead to reserve it in advance.

The Union Oyster House is a veritable shrine to colonial American history and is extremely popular with bus groups. The walls are covered with Boston memorabilia and photographs of the many famous people who have stopped by to dine. Mary Ann Milano Picardi has commissioned much of the art, including the historic murals. And there's always a monster lobster in the water tank. "It's a memory-maker for families, something for the kids to talk about when they go home," says Jim Malinn. And there are flat-screen TVs above the bar

Vintage Spot: Faneuil Hall

BELL IN HAND TAVERN: EST. 1795

There are convincing cobblestones outside the door of this two century–old taproom located within Boston's Blackstone block, one of the oldest sections of the city.

Here families and tourists can be spotted taking a lunch break from walking the Freedom Trail that passes right by the door. In the evening, the Bell in Hand caters largely to the college crowd with flat-screen TVs on the wall, live DJ music for dancing on weekends, and nachos on the menu.

45 Union St.; (617) 227-2098; bellinhand.com

and a modern sound track plays in the background, incorporating the new with the old.

"The first thing you do in this industry is making sure people feel welcome. If you don't do that, nothing else matters," Jim says. "We are serving a New England dining experience enriched with history. Especially for visitors from other parts of the country, the Union Oyster House is awe-inspiring."

VOSE GALLERIES

238 NEWBURY ST. • BOSTON, MA 02116

(617) 536-6176 • VOSEGALLERIES.COM

More Than 175 Years Gathering Paintings

Few Boston art galleries can claim to have an international following, but Newbury Street's Vose Galleries is truly a big-league player.

In some ways the history of Vose Galleries mirrors the development of Boston as a leading cultural center in the mid- to late 19th century. Vose Galleries is the oldest family-owned art gallery in the country, established in 1841 when Joseph Vose purchased the Westminster Art Gallery in Providence, Rhode Island.

By the 1850s, Joseph Vose's son Seth expanded the small business from mostly an art supply store to selling paintings. Carey Vose, who along with her sister Elizabeth are the sixth generation of the Vose family to work in the gallery, describes how her great-great-grandfather developed relationships with some of the most prominent artists of the day, representing works by Albert Bierstadt, Martin Johnson Heade, and George Inness.

Seth Vose was one of the first American galleries to exhibit works by artists of the Barbizon School, a group of French artists devoted to depictions of landscapes and genre scenes of the French countryside. Carey says, "William Morris Hunt came into my great-great-grandfather's shop and looked behind the curtain and saw all the Corots and Millets, gave him a big hug, and said, 'We are of the same ilk!'"

"Seth Vose became enthralled with the French Barbizon paintings. But at that time, no one in New England was buying them. The Barbizons were way too progressive, too bohemian. In 1852 Seth organized a show of 30 works by Jean Corot and not one sold."

Barbizons were out of favor and underappreciated, yet Seth Vose was passionate about collecting them. By the 1870s and 1880s, American art patrons came around, and Vose Galleries was one of the primary sources in the US for the French paintings.

Vose Galleries first expanded into Boston, leasing a small space at the Boston Studio Building on Tremont Street in 1880. Later, Seth's son, Robert, decided to branch out, and in 1896 he established the Robert C. Vose Gallery on Arlington Street in Boston's Back Bay. "My great-great-grandfather was a real personality; he sold what was in vogue—everything from Old Masters, to French Barbizons, to English portraiture." Vose Galleries has been part of the history of the frame world as well. In 1917, Robert acquired the Carrig-Rohane frame shop, and as Carey puts it, "Those are Cadillac frames now." By 1924 the business had flourished and Robert moved the gallery to a four-story building with an elevator in Copley Square.

By the 1960s Carey's grandfather, Robert C. Vose Jr., and her father, Bill Vose, had joined the gallery. Vose Galleries changed its collecting focus and became known for its commitment to American paintings of the 18th, 19th, and early 20th centuries. "Those were the years that many museums were buying for their American collection. Before that, no one really cared about American art," Carey explains. Vose Galleries has advised many museum committees regarding acquisitions for their collections. "American art was my grandfather's passion and he influenced so many people. In those days, many of the curators and museum directors had gone to Harvard and had often visited here as students." Today, paintings from Vose Galleries hang in almost every major American museum.

Robert C. Vose Jr. bought the Newbury Street brownstone that is Vose Gallery's current home for $39,000 in 1960. "When my grandparents moved here, it was a pretty seedy neighborhood. Everyone said they paid too much. The building was in rough shape and it took two years to renovate it. The main level and basement were the gallery space, and my grandparents lived in the upstairs apartment for 30 years." Today the top floor is dedicated to the gallery's

Vintage Spots: Back Bay
SHREVE CRUMP & LOW: EST. 1796

One of the oldest jewelers in the country, Shreve's is where Boston's high society has always shopped for their baubles. The store has moved around the city over the years, most recently to a renovated brownstone on Newbury Street in 2012. Shreve's also has some surprising sports connections. In 1869 tennis player Dwight F. Davis commissioned Shreve's to create a trophy to be awarded for a new annual men's international team competition, which is now known as the Davis Cup. And in 1908 Shreve's designed baseball's Cy Young Award, presented each year to the best pitcher in the major leagues.

39 Newbury St.; (617) 267-9100; shrevecrumpandlow.com

contemporary division, which offers beautiful, high-quality art typically at more affordable prices. Vose has introduced a wide range of artists to the Boston art scene, like Joel Babb, known for his amazingly detailed bird's-eye-view paintings of Boston, and pastels by Liz Haywood Sullivan.

The houselike setting certainly lessens the intimidation factor. And like Carey, the staff at Vose is young and enthusiastic—and happy to let visitors browse. "Our clients aren't typically people walking in from the street, but our doors are always open for anyone to come in, including students," says Carey. "For novice buyers there is often a threshold fear, but once clients visit, we can help them find something in their price range."

Vose Galleries is truly a family affair. "My mother and father still work part-time in business along with me and my sister. It's been 10 years and I would say that we have all settled into our roles and have a very good working dynamic." Carey continues with a laugh, "I can't complain—I really have fabulous bosses and great coworkers.

"For my family, art has always been our livelihood, what we are passionate about. We still handle the best; we still get Winslow

Homers, we still get Mary Cassatt and other big names too. But our bread and butter are the New England names. Most of our clients live here and typically want New England scenes. We've tried going outside of New England and it just doesn't work. This is our formula. I guess there's something to be said for being the last bastion."

WALLY'S CAFE

427 MASSACHUSETTS AVE. • BOSTON, MA 02118

(617) 424-1408 • WALLYSCAFE.COM

Keeping Its Cool for More Than Six Decades

Opened in 1947, this tiny jazz club with its authentic speakeasy atmosphere attracts fans of every stripe and has a proud tradition of showcasing the best young, upcoming Boston jazz musicians.

Wally's is the last remaining South End jazz club and has three generations of roots in Boston. Founded in 1947 by Joseph L. "Wally" Wolcott, the club is currently owned and operated by the brothers Poindexter: Frank, Lloyd, and Paul, who are Wally's grandsons. Their mother, Elynor Walcott, inherited the club from her father—Wally lived to the ripe old age of 101—and still helps out. Frank says, "We've always run it as a family business. I remember working here when I was 8 years old, sorting beer bottles."

Wally was an immigrant from Barbados who arrived in Boston in 1910. He settled in the South End, which by the 1940s was home to a growing black middle class. In those days, the South End was in full swing, home to storied clubs like the Hi-Hat and the Savoy. Wally worked a number of odd jobs, eventually owning a few cabs. He opened Wally's Paradise, the city's first black-owned nightclub, with the backing of then-mayor James Michael Curley—who was one of Wally's regular fares and famously understood how to court votes from every constituency.

Frank is particularly proud of Wally's then-groundbreaking vision: "My grandfather went out to the schools—Harvard, Boston College, Northeastern, and Boston University—and handed out circulars to the students. Wally's was the first integrated club in Boston where black and white people could socialize together." During the 1940s and 1950s jazz greats like Charlie Parker and Billie Holiday played Wally's stage.

But jazz joints come and jazz joints go. Originally located at 428 Mass Ave., Wally's moved to its current digs in the first floor of a red-brick town house at 427 Massachusetts Ave. in 1979. Today Wally's is a proving ground for young jazz musicians, offering live music 365 nights a year. The club is mostly associated with the nearby Berklee College of Music, but Wally also hosts students from New England Conservatory and Boston Conservatory. Most of the acts are small combos and on any given night you might encounter traditional swing, blues, Latin, or contemporary jazz.

Frank explains, "The older guys come in and feed off the energy of the kids, and the kids get the learning experience of how to control a music set. The musician's craft also takes business, communication, and organizational skills. The students learn how to create networks, how to run things, and how to interact with each other. At Wally's, the students meet people and they get gigs."

Weekend jam sessions often feature memorable performances by musicians dropping in, blending their own styles and improvising. On other nights you never know who will show up for a surprise appearance—recently Soulive did an impromptu late-night set.

"We have had some of the most talented musicians from around the world to play here," says Frank. Wally's has far-reaching connections in both the Boston and national jazz scenes. Grammy award-winning producer Jeff Bhasker played Wally's for years while a student at Berklee, as did Berklee alum and Grammy-winning musician Esperanza Spalding.

There is never a cover charge and if the sound is good, people often wander in off the street. There are just a handful of tables, so late night, you'll likely be cooling your heels at the bar. And despite "cafe" as part of the name, there isn't any food served to go along with your drinks.

There is a real sense of a musical community at Wally's. Here, an immigrant's dream became one of the country's greatest jazz clubs. Of his family's legacy, Frank says, "I love America. I love meeting all these people from around the world. And I get to hear great music all day long. Wally's is all right."

WARREN TAVERN

2 PLEASANT ST. • BOSTON, MA 02129

(617) 241-8142 • WARRENTAVERN.COM

One of Paul Revere's Favorite Bars

*J*ust down the street from the Bunker Hill Monument, this was once the watering hole of George and Paul (Washington and Revere) and now rallies bustling crowds of tourists and after-work locals for well-poured pints of beer, and classic pub food like fish and chips, steak tips, and burgers.

Dating from 1780, the Warren Tavern was established by Eliphalet Newell, who named the tavern in honor of Dr. Joseph Warren, a

prominent physician and American patriot who died a young hero during the 1775 Battle of Bunker Hill. Actually fought on nearby Breed's Hill, the Battle of Bunker Hill was the first major battle of the Revolutionary War. It was a Pyrrhic victory for the British, who took the fight, but the colonists took the momentum.

The British burned down the original tavern on this site during the battle. In colonial times, taverns were not just for drinking and socializing, but an integral part of daily life as a place to transact business and for political meetings. "This was one of the first buildings that was rebuilt in Charlestown after the Revolutionary War. Our Founding Fathers knew what their priorities were," jokes John Harnett, the Warren Tavern's general manager for the past 14 years.

Warren Tavern's historical claims are legitimate. King Solomon's Lodge, the Masonic Temple of which Paul Revere was a founding member and eventually Grand Master, was established at the Warren Tavern in 1786. "They used to have their meetings here and record notes that included who participated in every toast, so we know that George Washington and Paul Revere were really here in this building," explains John.

The Warren Tavern has had several incarnations and has changed hands many times over its long life span. Since 2006, Irishmen Pat O'Sullivan and Thomas Devlin have owned the Warren Tavern. Besides a tavern, the building has been a bakery, a men's club, a warehouse, and—reportedly—a speakeasy during Prohibition. In the 1960s, when the neighborhood was in decline, the building was closed altogether, the structure an eyesore that was scheduled for demolition in 1970. But the tavern was saved by the Boston Redevelopment Authority, which designated the site as a historical landmark. Today the Warren Tavern's rebuilt clapboard exterior, low exposed beamed ceiling, and stone fireplace reflect the building's 18th-century origins.

Like a lot of places in New England that have seen a lot of history, the Warren Tavern is also reputed to be haunted. Says John, "I've heard things late at night, the lights sometimes flicker off and on, and chairs have been moved."

Traditionally a working-class Irish enclave, since the 1980s white-collar professionals—lured by the neighborhood's proximity to Boston—began to snap up Charlestown's redbrick town homes at bargain prices. "Over the years, the area has changed quite a bit," says John. "Besides tourists, a huge base of our customers are longtime residents, but the neighborhood has been gentrified and now a lot of our customers are new families with kids. We just open the doors and people come in. Business has been good."

WINMIL FABRICS

111 CHAUNCY ST. • BOSTON, MA 02111

(617) 542-1815

Every Imaginable Fabric at a Discount

*L*ocated at the edge of Chinatown, Winmil is the last major surviving fabric store in downtown Boston. A smaller number of
people who sew their own clothes and rising rents have closed

all the other fabric stores in Boston's once-thriving Garment District, which throughout much of the 1900s consisted of several dozen clothing manufacturing plants, factory lofts, and warehouses along Chauncy, Essex, Beach, and Kneeland Streets.

Started by father and son Mel and Howard Held in 1969, this family business is stocked floor to ceiling with affordable fabrics and notions as well as unusual and high-end textiles you won't find at the national chain fabric stores.

Whereas many fabric shops can feel cluttered and chaotic, Winmil is large and bright and maintains an orderly feel. The store's biggest sellers are its quilting cottons, dress fabrics, and men's wool suiting. Big shipments come in nearly every two weeks but there are new things on the floor almost daily.

Originally located around the corner in a 1,000-square-foot Essex Street storefront, Winmil began as a wholesale fabric business supplying suburban fabric stores. Says Howard, "Back in the 1960s and '70s

nearly every town around Boston had one or two fabric shops." But Winmil always kept its doors open for walk-in customers, eventually converting to a strictly retail operation when it moved to its current Chauncy Street address in 1973. Initially Winmil occupied the basement, then moved upstairs after purchasing its current 4,000-square-foot street-level space in 1976.

Howard's father helped run the business for 15 years before retiring in 1974. Today the driving force behind Winmil Fabrics is another Held team: Howard along with his wife, Marilyn. Married to Howard for more than 45 years, Marilyn began working at Winmil in 1976. She explains, "We have two children and when our youngest was 4 years old, I decided to come and learn the business." In describing their working relationship, Marilyn says, "We've learned a lot about compromise. Very rarely do we argue because we each know what we are good at. Howard's expertise is negotiating what we pay for the fabrics with the connections and sources that we have in the industry. My expertise is knowing what will and will not sell."

Howard attributes much of Winmil's success to the uniqueness of their stock. By buying directly from fabric mills, Winmil has access to hundreds of manufacturer sample pieces: luminous silks, handkerchief linens, and opulent jacquards all offered at a steep discount. "Much of what you find in our store, you can't get anywhere else," says Marilyn.

The store has become a gathering place for customers who come in frequently each week during their lunch hour or after work. Marilyn adds, "We have a very loyal customer base. Almost every day, we get one or two people who come in and share with Howard and I stories of how they shopped here with their mom or grandmother. We have a hard time even thinking of retiring because of our customers."

According to Marilyn, recently there has been resurgence in sewing. Winmil is popular among everyone from neophyte home sewers to budget-stretched fashion students to Boston's top interior designers. "Many of our customers are international. They sewed where they came from and continue to do it today," explains Marilyn. Winmil also gets a lot of travelers who buy fabric to take home where labor is cheaper and have it made into a garment. "Fabric is a big thing for international visitors to give as a gift." Marilyn turns to Howard and asks, "Wouldn't you say that you can find a Winmil bag almost anywhere in the world?" Howard can only agree.

Appendix A:

FEATURED PLACES BY CATEGORY

Delicatessens
Rubin's Kosher Restaurant, 131

Doughnuts
Betty Ann Food Shop, 1

Entertainment
Club Passim, 37
Wally's Café, 165

Fabric Stores
Winmil Fabrics, 172

German Restaurant
Jacob Wirth, 76

Grocery Stores
Cardullo's, 24
Salumeria Italiana, 134
Syrian Grocery Importing
    Co., 150

Italian Restaurant
Caffe Vittoria, 21
Galleria Umberto, 56
Mamma Maria, 97
Regina Pizzeria, 123
Santarpio's Pizza, 137

Hot Dogs
Sullivan's, 147

Ice Cream
Ron's Gourmet Ice Cream, 128

Jewelry
E.B. Horn, 50

Leather Goods
Helen's Leather Shop, 69

Memorials
Deveney & White, 40

Pianos
M. Steinert & Sons, 104

Pizza
Galleria Umberto, 56
Regina Pizzeria, 123
Santarpio's Pizza, 137

Records
Cheapo Records, 30

Restaurants
Cafe Algiers, 17
Caffe Vittoria, 21
China Pearl, 33
Doyle's Cafe, 43
Durgin Park, 46
Frank's Steakhouse, 53
Galleria Umberto, 56
Gerard's Adams Corner, 59
Jacob Wirth, 76
J.J. Foley's, 80
Mamma Maria, 97
Mr. Bartley's, 100
No Name Restaurant, 112
Parker's Restaurant at the
    Omni Parker House Hotel, 115
Regina Pizzeria, 123
Rubin's Kosher Restaurant, 131
Santarpio's Pizza, 137
South Street Diner, 140

Appendix B:

FEATURED PLACES BY NEIGHBORHOOD/CITY

Appendix C:

FEATURED PLACES BY YEAR OF ORIGIN

1927: The Taj Boston, 154

1929: Caffe Vittoria, 21

1930: Phillips Candy House, 119

1931: Betty Ann Food Shop, 1

1932: Bova Bakery, 5

1932: Harvard Book Store, 65

1938: Frank's Steakhouse, 53

1939: Irving's Toy & Card Shop, 73

1940: Syrian Grocery Importing Co., 150

1946: Deveney & White, 40

1947: South Street Diner, 140

1947: Wally's Café, 165

1948: Bromfield Pen Shop, 13

1948: Charles Street Supply, 27

1950: Cardullo's, 24

1951: Sullivan's, 147

1952: Ron's Gourmet Ice Cream, 128

1954: Cheapo Records, 30

1958: Club Passim, 37

1960: Mr. Bartley's, 100

1961: China Pearl, 33

1962: Salumeria Italiana, 134

1965: Sterlingwear of Boston, 143

1970: Cafe Algiers, 17

1970: Helen's Leather Shop, 69

1971: Winmil Fabrics, 172

1972: Galleria Umberto, 56

1973: Mamma Maria, 97

1977: Gerard's Adams Corner, 59

1976: Kenmore Army Navy, 87

1978: Kupel's Bakery, 90

Photo Credits

All photos are courtesy of their establishments:

Index